Reprints of Economic Classics

SCOTTISH ECONOMIC LITERATURE

TO 1800

SCOTTISH

ECONOMIC LITERATURE

TO 1800

A LIST OF AUTHORITIES

PREPARED BY

WILLIAM R. SCOTT

[1911]

REPRINTS OF ECONOMIC CLASSICS

AUGUSTUS M. KELLEY · PUBLISHERS

NEW YORK 1971

First Edition 1911
(Glasgow & Edinburgh: William Hodge & Company, 1911)

REPRINTED 1971 BY
AUGUSTUS M. KELLEY • PUBLISHERS
REPRINTS OF ECONOMIC CLASSICS
New York New York 10001

. . . .

I S B N 0-678-00717-9
L C N 77-125362

. . . .

PRINTED IN THE UNITED STATES OF AMERICA
by SENTRY PRESS, NEW YORK, N. Y. 10019

Scottish Exhibition of National History, Art and Industry, Glasgow, 1911.

History, Historical Art and Historical Exhibits.

Sub-Section—EARLY ECONOMIC LITERATURE.

Committee—{ PROFESSOR WILLIAM SMART, M.A., D.Phil., LL.D.
W. R. SCOTT, M.A., D.Phil., Litt.D. }

SCOTTISH ECONOMIC LITERATURE TO 1800:

A LIST OF AUTHORITIES PREPARED FOR THE COMMITTEE

BY

W. R. SCOTT, M.A., D.Phil., Litt.D.,

Lecturer in Political Economy in the University of St. Andrews.

GLASGOW AND EDINBURGH:

WILLIAM HODGE AND COMPANY.

PREFACE.

There could be no stronger proof of the interest in the development of commerce in Scotland than the desire of the Exhibition of 1911 to form a sub-section for early economic literature. It is only recently that scholars have begun to devote themselves to the study of Scottish industry in early times apart from that of England, and for this reason it is impossible to say at present what printed authorities are available. Moreover, an exhibition of a selection of books would be unsatisfactory, since, at any given time, only a few of these could be shown, and the visitor could not see more than a page or two of each. To make this section as useful as possible, an attempt has been made to provide in the following pages a list of the chief sources of information concerning the early condition of trade in Scotland and the theories that were formed to explain its nature. No doubt there may be some difference of opinion as to what exactly is early economic literature. Generally speaking, any work written before Adam Smith's *Wealth of Nations* might be so classed. Then, in order to show the change effected by this book, the list has been continued so as to extend to 1800. It cannot be claimed that the titles mentioned below are complete; no doubt subsequent research will result in the discovery of many new authorities, but the works mentioned will suffice to provide material for at least the beginning of most investigations relating to economic subjects up to the end of the eighteenth century. How fruitful this field is likely to be may be gathered from what has recently been accomplished. There was the printing in 1896 by Professor Cannan of Adam Smith's lectures, delivered in 1763 (see below, No. 479). Then, as relating to the phenomena of industry and related subjects, there have appeared two books on the Scottish staple, the memorandum on the *History of the Scots Poor Laws prior to* 1845, in the Poor Law Commission's Report on Scotland, *the Records of a Scottish cloth manufactory at New Mills, Haddingtonshire,* 1681-1703, Miss Keith's *Commercial Relations of England and Scotland*, 1603-1707, as well as other contributions that might be mentioned.

With reference to the object in view, it has been decided to divide up the whole list into convenient periods, in each of which the books are arranged chronologically in respect to the time at which they were written as nearly as possible. It fortunately happens that in most cases the titles of the books are sufficiently detailed to afford some idea of the general nature of the contents. In a few cases, where this was not so, brief notes have been added. Then, to make the list as useful as possible, cases where rare tracts have been reprinted are noted.

The Committee begs to thank most cordially the libraries and individuals who have contributed to the success of this sub-section by the loan of books, many of which are of the greatest rarity. In this connection special thanks are due to the University Court of St. Andrews, the Signet Library, and Mr. J. J. Spencer.

WILLIAM SMART.
W. R. SCOTT.

THE MEDIÆVAL PERIOD.

DURING this period it would be misleading to expect to find any considerable body of information relating to the economic condition of the country in a specialised form. In Scotland during the Middle Ages there were two great centres of practical activity, namely, the burghs and the Church, and it is fortunate that a great mass of valuable material relating to both has been preserved, and, through the agency of various societies, much of it has been printed. Indeed, in some respects Scotland is exceptionally fortunate, since the earliest regulations extant, relating to the mediæval management of the commerce of towns in Great Britain, namely, the *Leges Burgorum* and the *Statuta Gildæ* of Berwick (Nos. 1 and 7) are both Scottish. Then the records of the burghs are very full, and copious extracts from these have been published, which give an immense amount of light on the type of industry in the towns (Nos. 2-5, 16-21, 24, 26, 29, 30, 35, 36, 38, 39, 41, 42, 44-50). Moreover, the system of federation of the burghs has resulted in all important questions having been discussed at the Convention, and its records are both valuable and interesting (No. 10). On the other hand, the predominance of the Church in rural districts makes its documents the great source of information on agriculture and life in the country. Various valuations and rentals of Church lands show changes in their productiveness, and afford some index as to the methods of husbandry and stock raising (Nos. 9, 11, 12, 23, 32, 33). Much is to be learnt of the trade and industry of both town and country from the Acts of Parliament and of the Privy Council. The former have been printed,* while a selection from the latter has appeared in Chambers's *Domestic Annals of Scotland*. These and other documents relating to the coinage and mining have been issued and edited by Mr. Cochran-Patrick (Nos. 6, 15). At such an early period much further information on foreign trade is scarcely to be expected, yet two important special works deserve notice, the one a collection of the concessions granted to Scottish merchants at

* *Acts of the Parliaments of Scotland.*

Vere, in the Netherlands (No. 37), and the other the papers of Andrew Halyburton, who was the conservator of the staple from 1492-1503 (No. 31). Further, it is surprising how much information can be collected upon minor economic inquiries. To take only one instance, that of the prices of commodities: a search through the various burgh records and those of the Convention would result in the accumulation of a great bulk of transactions, and in addition to that there are the Exchequer Rolls (No. 8), a curious note of the pay of English soldiers in Scotland in 1355 (No. 14), the cost of salmon for the Royal table, 1511-53 (No. 34), and a long run of the rates for cattle and grain at Aberdeen (No. 22). It is unnecessary to add that the fluctuations of the coinage have to be taken into account in dealing with results of this kind.

---

1 Ancient laws and customs of the Burghs of Scotland, 1124-1424.
(Printed by the Scottish Burgh Records Society, 1868.)

2 Charters and other documents relating to the Royal Burgh of Stirling, A.D. 1124-1705. 3 vols. 4° Glasgow 1884-9.

3 Charters and other documents relating to the Burgh of Glasgow, 1175-1707.
(Printed by the Scottish Burgh Records Society, 1897-1908.)

4 Charters of the Royal Burgh of Ayr [1202-1715]. 4° Edinburgh 1883.

5 Muniments of the Royal Burgh of Irvine [1205-1745].
(Printed by the Ayrshire and Galloway Archæological Association, 1890-1)

6 Early records relating to mining in Scotland [1219-1683].
(Edited by R. W. Cochran-Patrick, 1878.)

7 Statuta gildæ apud Berwicum facta [? 1249-1294].
(Printed in *The Guildry of Edinburgh*, by James Colston, 1887; also in No. 1.)

8 Rotuli scaccarii regum Scotorum. The Exchequer Rolls of Scotland, 1264-1600.
(Publications of the Stationery Office—in progress.)

9 Taxa et decimæ ecclesiarum et decanatuum ac monasteriorum diversorum in Scocia [? 1272-90].
(Printed by the Surtees Society in *The Priory of Coldingham*, 1841.)

10 Records of the Convention of the Royal Burghs of Scotland, with extracts from other records relating to the affairs of the Burghs of Scotland [1295-1711].

(Printed by the Scottish Burgh Records Society, 1866-80.)

11 Rentale antiquum de redditibus tenementis, etc., in Scocia. [*Circ.* 1298.]

(Printed by the Surtees Society in *The Priory of Coldingham*, 1841.)

12 Valuation of the Scottish bishopricks according to the old extent. [? Early cent. xiv.]

(Printed by the Maitland Club in *Illustrations of Scottish History*, 1834.)

13 The accounts of the Great Chamberlains of Scotland, and some other officers of the Crown, rendered at the Exchequer, 1326-1453.

(Printed by the Bannatyne Club, 1817-36.)

14 Roll of payments due to the garrisons in Scotland in possession of the English in the year 1355.

(Printed by the Maitland Club in *Illustrations of Scottish History*, 1834.)

15 Records of the coinage of Scotland from the earliest period [1357] to the Union.

(Edited by R. W. Cochran-Patrick, 1876.)

16 Royal Acts and statutes granted to the burgesses of Dundee, 1364-1592.

(Edited by Alex. J. Warden in *Burgh Laws of Dundee*, 1872.)

17 Extracts from the council register of the Burgh of Aberdeen, 1398-1570.

(Printed by the Spalding Club, 1844-8.)

18 Register of burgesses of guild and trade of the Burgh of Aberdeen, 1399-1631.

(Printed by the New Spalding Club—*Miscellany*, i., 1890.)

19 Guildry records of Aberdeen, 1399-1526.

(Printed in *The Guildry of Edinburgh*, by James Colston, 1887.)

20 Extracts from the records of the Burgh of Edinburgh, 1403-1589.

(Scottish Burgh Records Society, 1867-72.)

21 Proceedings of the gild court at Ayr, 1428-31.

(Printed in *Transactions of Ayr and Wigtown Archæological Association*, i.)

22 **An account of the antiquities of the City of Aberdeen, with the price of grain and cattle from the year 1435 to 1591.**
8° Edinburgh, n.d.

23 Rental book of the Cistercian Abbey of Cupar-Angus, with the breviary of the register [1443-1538].
(Printed by the Grampian Club, 1879-80.)

24. Extracts from the records of the Burgh of Peebles, 1456-1710.
(Printed by the Scottish Burgh Records Society, 1872.)

25 Retour of the lands of Wedderburn, 1469.
(Printed in *The Scottish Antiquary*, vii.)

26 Records of the Burgh of Prestwick, in the sheriffdom of Ayr, 1470-1732.
(Printed by the Maitland Club, 1834.)

27 Compota thesaurariorum regum Scotorum. Accounts of the Lord High Treasurer of Scotland, 1473-1541.
(Publications of the Stationery Office—in progress.)

28 The retour and royal warrant of taxation of the lands in the sheriffdom of Edinburgh, 1479.
(Printed by the Bannatyne Club—*Miscellany*, iii., 1855.)

29 The duties of the customes of this burgh [Edinburgh] of auld.
[? 1482.]
(Printed in *Extracts rrom the Records of the Burgh of Edinburgh*, 1403-1528—Burgh Records Society, 1869.)

30 Extracts from the records of the Burgh of Lanark, 1488-1722.
(Printed by the Scottish Burgh Records Society, 1873.)

31 Ledger of Andrew Halyburton, conservator of the privileges of the Scotch nation in the Netherlands, 1492-1503.
(Printed 1867.)

32 Liber protocollorum M. Cuthberti Simonis notarii publici et scribæ capituli Glasguensis, A.D. 1499-1513.
(Printed by the Grampian Club, 1875.)

33 Rental book of the Diocese of Glasgow, A.D. 1509-1570.
(Printed by the Grampian Club, 1875.)

34 Prices of salmon purchased for the Sovereigns of Scotland, 1511-53.
(Printed in *The Scottish Antiquary*, vii.)

35 Proceedings of the nine incorporated trades of Dundee, 1514-1839.
(Edited by Alex. J. Warden in *Burgh Laws of Dundee*, 1872.)

36 The Perth Hammermen Book, 1518-68.
(Edited by C. A. Hunt, Perth, 1889.)

37 Grants, &c., by Campvere to Scottish merchants [1539-1676].
(Printed in *The Privileges of the Scottish Burrows*, by W[illiam] B[lack], Edinburgh, 1707; *An Account of the Scotch Trade in the Netherlands*, London, 1776; *Bijdragen tot de Geschiedenis van den Schotschen Stapel te Vere*, by J. W. Perrels, 1903-5; *The Scottish Staple at Vere*, by J. Davidson and A. Gray, London, 1909.)

38 Edinburgh records. The burgh accounts, 1544-67.
(Printed by the Scottish Burgh Records Society, 1899.)

39 The Baxter Books of St. Andrews [1548-1861].
(Edited by J. H. Macadam, 1903.)

40 Burgh laws enacted at the head courts, composed of the provost, magistrates, dean of guild, and town council, and of the nine deacons of trades. Drawn furth of ye actis and statutis of yis brugh [Dundee], 1550-1694.
(Edited by Alex. J. Warden in *Burgh Laws oj Dundee*, 1872.)

41 Extracts from the accounts of the Burgh of Peebles, 1554-1661.
Printed in *Charters and Documents relating to the Burgh of Peebles*, 1165-1710—Burgh Records Society, 1872.)

42 Extracts from the accounts of the Common Good of various burghs in Scotland relative to payments for schools and schoolmasters between the years 1557 and 1634.
(Printed in *The Miscellany of the Maitland Club*, ii., Part i.)

43 Margill, Jacques, and Bellenden, Jean. Discours particulier d'Escosse : escrit par commandement et ordonnance, 11 Janier, 1559.
(Printed by the Bannatyne Club, 1824.)

44 Acts, statutes, and proceedings of the guildry incorporation of Dundee, 1570-1846.
(Edited by Alex. J. Warden in *Burgh Laws of Dundee*, 1872.)

45 Burgh records of the City of Glasgow, 1573-81.
(Printed by the Maitland Club, 1832.)

46 Extracts from the records of the Burgh of Glasgow, 1573-1738.
(Printed by the Scottish Burgh Records Society, 1876-1909.)

47 Extracts from the minute books of the Weavers' Corporation of Galashields, 1574-1692.

(Printed in the *Publications of the Hawick Archæological Society*, vol. viii.)

48 Constitutions and bye-laws of the guild court of Edinburgh, 1584.

(Printed in *The Guildry of Edinburgh*, by James Colston, 1887.)

49 Acts and ordinances of the seven incorporated trades of Aberdeen, 1599.

(Printed in *Merchant and Craft Guilds*, by Ebenezer Bain, 1887.)

50 Dumbarton burgh records, 1627-1746.

(Printed by the Scottish Burgh Records Society, 1860.)

THE MODERN PERIOD TO 1695.

It may have been noticed that in the mediæval period all the books mentioned have been printed at a later date. Towards the close of the sixteenth century printed matter, relating to trade and the coinage, began to appear. This method was found convenient in giving publicity to Acts of Parliament and of the Privy Council, and, since the former are accessible in the collection of statutes, it is not necessary to include them in the ensuing list. The earliest important printed works were those issued in support of the colonising of New Scotland or Nova Scotia between 1620 and 1630 (Nos. 67, 69, 72, 74), in which one notes the presence of the mercantilist view of colonies as an outlet from surplus production from the home market. Coinage continues to occupy the attention both of the Government and merchants, while towards the end of the period banking and paper money begin to be discussed (Nos. 120, 122-3, 127, 133-5). After 1680 there was a considerable revival of manufactures, and the original articles of companies for making linen and paper, dated 1694 and 1695, will be noted (Nos. 128, 129), also the recently discovered minutes of a cloth factory, 1681 to 1703 (No. 109), as well as a tract, printed in 1683 (No. 110), which was intended to secure public support for the scheme, and which represents the contemporary point of view on foreign trade, with the usual arguments towards securing a favourable balance and the attracting of bullion or the prevention of the export of it. Finally, in 1695 there came the culmination of the time of activity in the foundation of the Bank of Scotland (No. 135) and of the Darien Company. Since the literature relating to the latter is somewhat extensive, a selection from it will be given separately.

Regarding the material more in detail, trade in general is dealt with after the Restoration in Nos. 87, 91, and 93, more especially in relation to Scotland's commercial grievances against England, and also from various points of view in Nos. 106, 111, 119, 125, 126, 130. Tracts relating to manufactures begin to appear towards the end of the period (Nos. 96, 107-110, 128, 129). A mention of the trade of making golf balls, with details of the industry, between

1639 and 1654 is curious (No. 77). Agriculture and the cattle trade will be found described in Nos. 51, 58, 73, 75, 78; shipping and foreign trade in Nos. 53, 55, 56, 57, 88. Attention was also paid to fishing, *e.g.*, Nos. 52, 86, 132. Besides the work on mining already mentioned (No. 6), there are two others that are important for different reasons. One (No. 98) was printed as early as 1672, which, amongst miscellaneous problems in physics, describes the methods of coal mining then in vogue, and the situation of the chief pits. Another work, written in 1619, but printed in 1825, shows that gold mining was once a Scottish industry of some importance (No. 65). Prices of commodities and payments for services will be found comparatively well represented (Nos. 54, 60, 62, 64, 68, 71, 73, 75, 76, 81, 84, 89, 97, 99, 100, 103, 116-118), as are also topics relating to the Revenue, taxation, the Customs, and Excise (Nos. 53, 61, 78, 80, 82, 83, 85, 89, 92, 94, 95, 101, 102, 104, 105, 112, 113, 121, 124, 131). *Note.*—Nos. 2-6, 8, 10, 15, 18, 24, 26, 30, 35, 37, 39, 40-42, 44, 46, 47, 50 extend into this period.

---

51 Documents connected with the general intercourse of trade between the Highlands and Lowlands, and more particularly the trade of cattle dealing in the Highlands and the Isles, 1565-1622.

(Printed in *Publications of the Iona Club*, xii.)

52 Documents illustrative of the fisheries in the West Highlands and the Isles, 1566-1635.

(Printed in *Publications of the Iona Club*, ix.)

53 Ane buik conteanand the intrassis of schippis dischaergeand at ye port of Dundie beginning in ye moneth of November in Anno Dni. 1580.

(Printed in *Compt Buik of David Wedderburne*—Scottish History Society, 1898.)

54 Inventory of goods, 1583.

(Printed in *The Scottish Antiquary*, i.)

55 Account of the quantity of lead exported from Scotland, 1585-90.

(Printed in *Analecta Scotica*, i.)

56 The compt-buik of David Wedderburne, merchant of Dundee, 1587-1630.

(Printed by the Scottish History Society, 1898.)

57. Inuarde custumes. The valuation and prices of merchandries brocht within this realme, quhairof xiid. for ilk pund of the price theairof suld be takin up in name of custume, 22 Maij, 1597.

(Printed in *Ledger of Andrew Halyburton.*)

58 The rentaill of the lordschipe of Huntlye, alias Strauthbogye, maid be the richt noble and michty George, Marquis of Huntly, Erll of Engzie, Lord Gordon and Badzenoche, &c., for his lordschipis landis followinge, conform to the sett maid at Witsonday, ane thousand and sax hundrethe yeirs.

(Printed in *The Miscellany of the Spalding Club*, iv.)

59 The court book of the Barony of Urie, in Kincardineshire, 1604-1747.

(Printed by the Scottish History Society, 1892.)

60 Household account of Ludovick, Duke of Lennox, when Commissioner to the Parliament of Scotland, Anno 1607.

(Printed in *The Miscellany of the Maitland Club*, Part i., 1833.)

61 The rates and valuations of merchandizes and goods imported within the Kingdom of Scotland. 4° [no title page] 1611.

62 A Haddington surgeon's account, 1611.

(Printed in *The Scottish Historical Review*, ii.)

63 Extracts from the court books of the Baronies of Skene, Leys, and Whitehaugh, 1613-87.

(Printed by the Spalding Club—*Miscellany* v., 1852.)

64 The account book of Sir John Foulis of Ravelston, 1617-1707.

(Printed by the Scottish History Society, 1894.)

65 Atkinson, Stephen. The discoverie and historie of the gold mynes in Scotland; written in the year 1619.

(Printed by the Bannatyne Club, 1825.)

66 A perfect description of the people and country of Scotland, 1619.

(Reprinted under the title of *A Satire against Scotland*, by the Abbotsford Club—*Miscellany* i., 1837.)

67 [Mason, Captain John]. A briefe discourse of the New-found land, with the situation, temperature and commodities thereof, inciting our nation to goe forward in that hopefull plantation begunne. 4° Edinburgh 1620.

(Reprinted by the Bannatyne Club, 1867.)

68 The testament testamentar, and inventar of the guidis, geir, somes of money and debs pertening to umquhile Richard Lausone, merchand-burges of Edinburgh, the tyme of his deceis, quha deceist upon the day of September, 1622 zeiris.

(Printed by the Bannatyne Club—*Miscellany*, iii., 1855.)

69 Alexander, Sir William. An encouragement to colonies.
4° London 1624.

(Reprinted by the Bannatyne Club, 1867.)

70 Hunter, Alexander. A treatise of weights, mets, and measures of Scotland, with their quantities, and true foundation, and sundry profitable observations arising upon everie one of them together with the art of metting, measuring, and computing all sorts of land, with diverse tables.
4° Edinburgh 1624.

71 The testament testamentar and inventar of the guidis and geir, etc., pertening to umquhile George Heriot, jeweler to the Kingis Majestie, 1624.

(Printed in *The Miscellany of the Maitland Club*, iii., Part ii.)

72 [Gordon, Sir Robert, of Lochinvar.] Encouragements for such as shall have intention to bee under-takers in the new plantation of Cape-Briton, now New-Galloway, in America.
4° Edinburgh 1625.

(Reprinted by the Bannatyne Club, 1867.)

73 R. C. Mossman, F.R.S.E. On the price of wheat at Haddington from 1627 to 1897.

(Reprinted from *The Accountants' Magazine*, 1900.)

74 Alexander, Sir William. The mapp and description of New-England; together with a discourse of plantation, and collonies: also a relation of the nature of the climate and how it agrees with our owne country, England. How neere it lyes to New-found-land, Virginia, Nova Francia, Canada, and other parts of the West Indies. 4° London 1630.

(Reprinted by the Bannatyne Club, 1867.)

75 The book of the annualrentaris and wedsettaris within the schirrefdome of Aberdein, 1633.

(Printed in *The Miscellany of the Spalding Club*, iii.)

76 General tax roll of 1633.

(Printed in *Revenue of the Scottish Crown*, 1681, edited by D. Murray Rose.)

77 Extracts from the minute book of the Craft of Shoe-makers in Canongate, Edinburgh, relating to the golf-ball makers of Leith, 1639-54.

(Printed in *The Scottish Antiquary*, x.)

78 Commission anent valuation of teinds [? 1642].

79 Extracts from the council register of the Burgh of Aberdeen, 1643-1747.

(Printed by the Scottish Burgh Records Society, 1871.)

80 Minutes of the Committee for loan monies and taxations of the shire of Aberdeen, 1643.

(Printed in *The Miscellany of the Spalding Club*, iii.)

81 Extracts from documents relating to servants' wages, 1650-89.

(Printed in *The Scottish Antiquary*, iv.)

82 Rules, orders, etc., anent the customs of Scotland.
4° Edinburgh 1656.

83 Tucker, Thomas. Report upon the settlement of the revenues of excise and customs in Scotland, A.D. 1656.

(Printed by the Bannatyne Club, 1824, also by the Scottish Burgh Records Society—*Miscellany*, 1881.)

84 Extracts from the account-book of Nicol Gairdiner, treasurer of the Burgh of Linlithgow for the year 1659.

(Printed in *Analecta Scotica*, i.)

85 Ressons humbly offered in the behalf of Scotland, concerning the exceeding great disproportions betwixt the assessments of that nation at 6000*l*. per mensen, and the assessment of England at 35,000*l*. monethly. s. sh. n.p. [1660.]

86 Smith, John. The trade and fishing of Great Britain, displayed, with a description of the islands of Orkney and Shetland
4° London 1661.

87 A short essay upon the disorders of Scotland [? 1661].

(Printed in *Miscellanea Aulica*, 1702.)

88 An memorial of the several services done to the Kings of France by the Scots with an inventar of the privileges granted to them by those Kings upon that account [? 1663].

(Printed in *The Privileges of the Royal Burrows*, by W[illiam] B[lack], Edinburgh, 1707.)

89 Excerpts from the Household Book of my Lord Archbishop of St. Andrews from 1663 to 1666.

(Printed in *The Miscellany of the Maitland Club*, ii., Part ii.)

90 Valuation of the shire of Wigtown made in 1667.

(Printed in *Publications of Ayrshire and Galloway Archæological Association*, vol. vi.)

91 A paper given in by the Scots Commissioners to the English Commissioners for adjusting the differences of trade between the two kingdoms, 21st January, 1667.

(Printed in *The History of the Union*, by Daniel de Foe; edited by G. Chalmers, 1786, Appendix No. 13.)

92 List of the fees and pensions granted to the officers of State and other servants of the Crown in Scotland, 1667-1699.

(Printed in *The Miscellany of the Maitland Club*, iii., Part i.)

93 The grievances of Scotland in relation to their trade with England. Sent up to the Council 3rd February, 1668.

(Printed in *Miscellanea Aulica*, 1702.)

94 Book of rates . . . on stockings and plaidings.
s. sh. Aberdeen 1670.

95 The rates of his Majestie's customes . . . for goods and merchandise imported or exported to and from the Kingdom of Scotland. . . . 8° Edinburgh 1670.

96 Letter and account James Marr, "clerk of the manufactorie att Air," concerning cloth sent to Sir William Bruce, 10th March, 1670.

(Printed in *The Scottish Antiquary*, i.)

97 The report of the surveyors of the wayis in Kirk-Listone Parish, within the sheriffdome of Edinburgh, 1670.

(Printed in *Analecta Scotica*, i.)

98 Sinclair, George, Professor of Philosophy, Glasgow. The Hydrostaticks; together with some miscellany observations, the last whereof is a short history of coal.
4° Edinburgh 1672.

99 Extracts from household accounts, 1674-5.

(Printed in *The Scottish Antiquary*, ii.)

100 The account book of Dame Erskine, 1678-9.

(Printed in *The Scottish Antiquary*, ix.)

101 Table of all the pettie customs in Aberdeen.
s. sh. [Aberdeen 1679.]

102 Table of all the dues payable to the Burgh of Aberdeen.
s. sh. [Aberdeen 1679.]

103 The diary and general expenditure book of William Cunningham of Craigends, Commissioner to the Convention of Estates and Member of Parliament for Renfrewshire, kept chiefly from 1673 to 1680.
(Printed by the Scottish History Society, 1887.)

104 Purves, Sir William. An accompt of his Majesties proper rentes arryseing from the few and blench duties of the severall landes holden few and blench of his Majestie in his Kingdom of Scotland [1681] with the deductiones, alterationes, and differences betwixt the present rentall and the former, preceeding King James of blissed memory his goeing into England in Anno 1603.
(Printed in a volume entitled *Revenue of the Scottish Crown*, edited by D. Murray Rose.)

105 The retoured dewties of the haill shyres [1681].
(Printed in *Revenue of the Scottish Crown.*)

106 Charters and Acts of Parliament in favour of the Merchant Company of Edinburgh [1681-1827].
(Printed in *Historical Notes regarding the Merchant Company of Edinburgh*, by Charles Lawson, 1862.)

107 Articles aggreed upon be the merchands erectors of the cloath manufactory at Newmilnes [1680-1].
(Printed by the Scottish History Society, 1905.)

108 A Memoriall concerning the cloath manufactory [at New Mills, Haddingtonshire 1681].
(Printed by the Scottish History Society, 1905.)

109 Book for the manufactories [being the minute book of the managers of the cloth manufactory at New Mills 1681-1703].
(Printed by the Scottish History Society, 1905.)

110 A representation of the advantages that would arise to this kingdom by the erecting and improving of manufactories, but more especially that of woollen cloth, with an answer to the objections against this last, and an account of its present state and success of the manufactory at Newmills for woollen cloath, serges, silk, and worsted stockings, and of the rules and methods observed by the undertakers in managing it, with proposals to such as shall be willing to join in that work. 4° Edinburgh 1683.

111 The sett or decreet arbitral of King James VI. of blessed memory deciding all deferences betwixt merchants and trades, anent the government of the City of Edinburgh as it is registrat in the books of the Council of Session and ratified in Parliament. 8° Edinburgh 1683.

112 Sufereinces for the excyses impositione. [Aberdeen 1683.]

113 Establishment for the pay of His Majesty's standing forces in the Kingdom of Scotland, 16th June, 1684.

(Printed in *The Miscellany of the Maitland Club*, iii., Part i.)

114 Proposals by Walter Gibson, merchant in Glasgow, to persons who wish to transport themselves to America, 1684.

115 Advertisement to all tradesmen and others, who are willing to transport themselves into the Province of New Jersey, in America, 1684.

(Nos. 114, 115 printed by the Bannatyne Club—*Miscellany*, iii., 1855.)

116 Papers referr'd to by the owners of the ships "Palm-tree" and "Patience." Fol. Edinburgh 1684.

117 Petition to the King's Advocate . . . for the ships "Palm-tree" and "Patience." Fol. Edinburgh 1684.

118 True state of the case of the two Danish ships, called the "Palm-tree" and "Patience." Fol. Edinburgh 1684.

119 [Skene, Alexander.] Memorialls for the government of the Royall Burghs in Scotland, by Philopoliteius. 8° Aberdeen 1685.

(Reprinted 1833 under title *An Ancient Account of the famous City of Aberdeen.*)

120 Information relating to the mint. Fol. [Edinburgh 1686.]

121 Table of the dues payable . . . in the bread and poultry mercat. [Edinburgh] 1686.

122 Table of the value of bullion in Scots money.

123 Table of the value of bullion (in standard silver). s. sh. [1687.]

124 [Savile, George, Marquis of Halifax.] The anatomy of an Equivalent. 4° n.p. [? 1689.]

(Reprinted in *State Tracts of the reign of Charles II.*; also in 1706, *vide* No. 329.)

125 Petty, Sir William. Several essays in political arithmetick. 8° London 1691.

(In *Political Arithmetick, or a Discourse concerning the extent and value of lands, people, buildings,* estimates are given of the population and wealth of Scotland.)

126 Register containing the state and condition of every burgh within the Kingdom of Scotland in the year 1692.

(Printed by the Scottish Burgh Records Society—*Miscellany*, 1881.)

127 C[hamberlain], H[ugh]. Papers relating to a bank of credit upon land security; proposed to the Parliament of Scotland. 4° [? Edinburgh] 1693.

128 Articles of agreement concluded, made and agreed on this twenty-eighth day of May in the year of our Lord 1694 between the Royal frie Burrows of Scotland, who shall be pleased to subscribe and be concerned in the Scots linen subscription book for the linen manufacture in that kingdom, on the one part, and Nicholas Dupin . . . in trust for the members, who shall be pleased to subscribe and be concerned in the aforesaid manufacture in England, of the other part. Edinburgh 1694

129 Articles concluded and agreed upon by the Society of the White Writing and Printing Paper Manufactory at Edinburgh, the 19th of August, 1695, in the terms whereof partners were to be assumed. 4° [Edinburgh 1695.]

130 Reasons general for a sumptuary law in Scotland. s. sh. n.p. [? 1694.]

131 Table of the impost and shoar dues of Aberdeen. s. sh. [Aberdeen 1695.]

132 A discourse concerning the fishery within the British seas, and other his Majesties dominions, and more especially as it relates to the Company of the Royal fishery of England: offered to consideration in order to subscriptions for raising a stock for carrying on the affairs thereof upon the terms proposed. 4° Edinburgh reprint 1695.

133 Memorial to the Privy Council anent the English clipt money. [Edinburgh 1695.]

134 [Mackenzie, George, Earl of Cromarty.] The mistaken advantage of raising money, discovered in a letter to a friend. 4° Edinburgh 1695.

135 Copy of a signature for a new bank. 4° [? Edinburgh 1695.]

THE MODERN PERIOD, THE DARIEN COMPANY, 1695 TO 1707.

THE industrial activity in Scotland in the seventeenth century culminated with the foundation of the Darien Company. Owing to the English Navigation Acts, it was not possible for Scotsmen to trade directly with the colonies, and it was logically necessary, to maintain the recent developments in production, that a wider market should be acquired. This was the inner meaning of the Darien scheme, from the commercial point of view. Scotland had staked much on the success of the project, and interest in it was so universal that during a few years an extensive Darien literature came into existence. The following titles of pamphlets and other publications constitute a selection from the whole, and a very full bibliography on this subject has been printed by the Edinburgh Bibliographical Society.

The publications that are most important may be divided into official ones, which will be found represented by Nos. 148-156, 157-172, 177, 182-185, 187A, 195-197, 200, and 203, and particularly by the collections Nos. 142 to 145. Then, immediately the company had been proposed, it was commented on from various points of view (Nos. 136-141, 146, 147). The site of the colony and the proceedings of the colonists were described (Nos. 173-176, 186, 187). Naturally, when the scheme had failed, there was a period of acute controversy as to the apportionment of the blame (Nos. 178-181, 188-194, 198-205, 211). Next come the reprisals of the company against the English East India Company, which led to the execution of Captain Green (Nos. 212-223). The final stage consisted in the relation of the company to the Act of Union (Nos. 225-233), to which may be added the subsequent adjustment of a claim by William Paterson (Nos. 234-239).

---

136 **Proposals for a fond to cary on a plantation, May 22, one thousand six hundred and ninty-five. Fol. [1695.]**

137 **Some considerations upon the late Act of Parliament of Scotland for constituting an Indian Company. In a letter to a friend. Fol. London 1695.**

138 Caveto Cavetote: being an answer to a late Scotch letter concerning a late Scotch Act, &c., by Tarpallian in Querpo.
Fol. [London 1695.]

139 The humble address of the Right Honourable the Lords Spiritual and Temporal, and Commons assembled, presented to his Majesty on the seventeenth of December, 1695.
Fol. London, reprinted at Edinburgh 1696.

(This was the beginning of the English Parliamentary Enquiry, reprinted in *Journals of the House of Commons.*)

140 A letter from a member of the Parliament of Scotland to his friend at London concerning their late Act for establishing a company of that kingdom tradeing to Africa and the Indies.
4° Reprinted Edinburgh 1695.

141 Some remedies to prevent the mischiefs from the late Act of Parliament made in Scotland in relation to the East India trade. s. sh. [? London 1695.]

142 A full and exact collection of all the considerable addresses, memorials, petitions, answers, proclamations, declarations, letters, and other publick papers relating to the company of Scotland trading to Africa and the Indies since the passing of the Act of Parliament, by which the said company was established in June, 1695, till November, 1700. 8° 1700.

143 The Darien papers: being a selection of original letters and official documents relating to the establishment of a colony at Darien by the company of Scotland trading to Africa and the Indies, 1695-1700.

(Printed by the Bannatyne Club, 1849.)

144 The Darien papers [a collection, consisting partly of printed matter, partly of MSS., at the Advocates' Library, comprising Acts of Parliament, minutes at meetings of the company or of committees, petitions, proclamations, letters, dispatches, reports, instructions, &c., 1695-1707].

145 The original papers and letters relating to the Scots company trading to Africa and the Indies [1696-9] 8° n.p. 1700.

145A —— A supplement to *The Original Papers and Letters* [1699-1700]. 8° n.p. 1700.

146 [K. C.] Some seasonable and modest thoughts partly occasioned by and partly concerning the Scots East India Company. Humbly offered to R. H., Esq., a member of the present Parliament. By an unfeigned and hearty lover of England. 4° Edinburgh 1696.

147 A letter from a gentleman in the country to his friend at Edinburgh: wherein it is clearly proved that the Scottish African and Indian Company is exactly calculated for the interest of Scotland. Fol. Edinburgh 1696.

148 Edinburgh, March 24th, 1696. At a meeting of the subscribers to the company of Scotland trading Africa and the Indies.

149 Edinburgh, April 3rd, 1696. At a general meeting of the company.

150 At a meeting of the committee appointed by the subscribers to the joint stock of the company . . . 17 April [1696].

151 Edinburgh, 17th day of April, 1696. At a general meeting of the company.

152 Constitutions of the company. Fol. [Edinburgh 1696.]

153 A list of the subscribers to the company of Scotland trading to Africa and the Indies. Taken in Edinburgh, etc., until the 21 of April, inclusive, 1696. Fol. [Edinburgh 1696.]

154 Edinburgh, 12th May, 1696. At a general meeting of the company. Fol. [Edinburgh 1696.]

155 Edinburgh, 20th May, 1696. At a court of directors of the company. s. sh. [Edinburgh 1696.]

156 Advertisement [by the directors of the Darien Co. for a supply of guns, swords, etc.]. Edinburgh, 20th May, 1696. s. sh. [1696.]

157 At Edinburgh, the 15th of June, 1696. The Council-General of the company.

158 At Edinburgh, the 9th day of July, 1696. Whereas the books of subscriptions to the company.

159 Edinburgh, 3rd of August, 1696. The above written act . . . was read . . . and the said Council-General doth hereby further enact and declare.

160 A perfect list of the several persons, residenters in Scotland, who have subscribed (with the respective sums) as adventurers in the joynt-stock of the company of Scotland, trading to Africa and the Indies. 8° Edinburgh 1696.

(Reprinted in *A History of William Paterson and the Darien Company*, by J. S. Barbour.)

161 A memorial given in to the Senate of the City of Hamburgh in French, faithfully translated into English. Fol. [1697.]

162 Edinburgh, the 12th day of March, 1698. The Indian and African Company of Scotland, having now in readiness ships and tenders . . . s. sh. Edinburgh 1698.

163 To . . . His Majesties High Commissioner . . . petition of the company [22nd July, 1698].

164 Information for Gaven Plummer, cashier to the Indian and African Company, against Lord Belhaven. Fol. [? 1698.]

165 Journal of the Scots African and Indian fleet, from the setting forth from Kirkcaldy, 8th July, 1698, to the arrival at the Bay of Darien, 1st November, 1699.

(Printed in *Analecta Scotica*, i.)

166 At a meeting of the Council-General of the company, 6th February, 1699.

167 The humble address of the Right Honourable the Lords Spiritual and Temporal in Parliament assembled, presented to His Majesty on Monday, the twelfth day of February, 1699. Fol.

168 At a Council-General of the company, 30th March, 1699. Fol.

169 Three memorials presented to His Majesty in May, 1699, by the Lord President of the Session and the Lord Advocate on behalf of the company.

(Printed in *Collection of Addresses, &c.*)

170 Proclamations by the Governors of Jamaica, Barbados, and New York, etc., prohibiting intercourse with the Scots colony at Darien, dated 8th, etc., April, 1699. Fol. Reprinted Edinburgh 1699.

(Reprinted in *Collection of Addresses, &c.*)

171 At a court of directors of the company . . . 18th day of April, 1699.

172 Petition to the King relative to His Majesty's orders to hold no intercourse with the Scots colony at Darien, and his Majestys answer [19th October and 2nd November, 1699]. s. sh. n.p. [1699].

(Reprinted in *Collection of Addresses, &c.*)

173 The History of Caledonia, or the Scots colony in Darien, in the West Indies, with an account of the manners of the inhabitants and the riches of the country. 8° London 1699.

(Reprinted in *A History of William Paterson and the Darien Company*, by J. S. Barbour.)

174 A short account from, and description of, the Isthmus of Darien, where the Scots collony are settled; with a particular map of the Isthmus and enterance to the river of Darien. According to our late news and Mr. Dampier and Mr. Wafer.
4° Edinburgh 1699.

175 A letter giving a description of the Isthmus of Darien (where the Scots colonie is settled;) from a gentleman who lives there at present. With an account of the fertilness of the soil, the quality of the air, the manners of the inhabitants, and the nature of the plants and animals, &c., and a particular mapp of the Isthmus and entrance to the river Darien.
4° Edinburgh 1699.

176 An abstract of a letter from a person of eminency and worth in Caledonia to a friend in Boston, New England.
Fol. Boston, reprinted Edinburgh 1699.

177 A letter from the Commission of the General Assembly . . . July 21, 1699, to the Scots colony of Caledonia.
4° [Edinburgh 1699.]

178 [Foyer, Rev. Archibald.] A defence of the Scots settlement at Darien, with an answer to the Spanish memorial against it, . . . to which is added a description of the country, and a particular account of the Scots colony.
8° Edinburgh 1699.

179 C P A short and impartial view of the manner and occasion of the Scots colony's coming away from Darien. In a letter to a Person of Quality. 4° Edinburgh 1699.

180 *The Defence of the Scots Settlement at Darien* [No. 178] answer'd, paragraph by paragraph, by Philo Britan.
8° London 1699

181 [? Ferguson, Robert.] A just and modest vindication of the Scots design for the having established a colony at Darien. With a brief display, how much it is their interest, to apply themselves to trade, and particularly to that which is foreign.
8° [Edinburgh] 1699.

182 At a Council-General of the company . . . 18th day of October, 1699

183. An express from the African and Indian Scots Company's fleet, landed at New-Edinburgh, in Caledonia.
s. sh. Edinburgh 1699.

184 An exact list of all the men, women, and boys that died on board the Indian and African Company's fleet during their voyage from Scotland to America and since their landing in Caledonia; together with a particular account of their qualities, and the several days of their deaths, and the respective distempers or accidents of which they died.
s. sh. Edinburgh 1699.

185 Caledonia. The declaration of the council constituted by the Indian and African Company of Scotland; for the government and direction of their colonies and settlements in the Indies [dated New-Edinburgh, December 18, 1699].
s. sh. Boston, reprinted Glasgow 1699.

(Reprinted in *A History of William Paterson and the Darien Company*, by J. S. Barbour.)

186 Wafer, Lionel. A new voyage and description of the Isthmus of America, giving an account of the author's abode there.
8° London 1699.

187 Information concernant l'affaire de Darien.
4° [? Paris ? 1699-1700.]

187A Proclamation anent petit[i]oning, 1699.

188 [Herries or Harris, Walter.] A defence of the Scots abdicating Darien; including an answer to *The Defence of the Scots Settlement there* [No. 178]. Authore Britanno sed Dunensi.
8° n.p. 1700.

189 An inquiry into the causes of the miscarriage of the Scots colony at Darien, or an answer to a libel entituled *A Defence of the Scots abdicating Darien* [No. 188]. 8° Glasgow 1700.

(Reprinted in *Collection of State Tracts relating to reign of William III.*)

190 [Herries or Harris, Walter.] A short vindication of Phil. Scot's *Defence of the Scots abdicating Darien* [No. 188]: being in answer to the challenge of the author of the *Defence* of that settlement to prove the Spanish title to Darien, by inheritance, marriage, donation, purchase, reversion, surrender, or conquest. With a prefatory reply to the false and scurrilous aspersions of the new author of *The just and modest vindication* [No. 181], &c. And some animadversions on the material part of it, relating to the title of Darien. 8° London 1700.

191 Certain propositions relating to the Scots plantations of Caledonia, and the national address for supporting thereof, briefly offered to the publick view, for removing of mistakes and prejudices. Fol. Glasgow 1700.

192 [A serious advice to the African and Indian Company, 1700.]

193 Scotland's present duty: or a call to the nobility, gentry, &c., in this land to be duely affected with, and vigorously to act for, our common concern in Caledonia, as a mean to enlarge Christ's Kingdom, &c. 4° n.p. 1700.

194 [Ridpath, George.] Scotland's grievances, relating to Darien, &c., humbly offered to the consideration of Parliament. 8° [? Edinburgh] 1700.

(Reprinted in *Collection of State Tracts relating to the reign of William III.*)

195 The humble representation and petition of the Council-General of the company [16th May, 1700].

(Reprinted in *Collection of Addresses, &c.*)

196 His Majesty's most gracious letter: directed to His Grace James, Duke of Queensberry, 1700.

197 The humble representation and petition of the Council-General of the company [28th October, 1700].

198 Considerations upon the question, whether the Parliament of Scotland should begin next session with asserting their right to Caledonia and the legality of our late settlement there. 12° [Edinburgh 1700.]

199 Scotland's right to Caledonia (formerly called Darien) and the legality of its settlement, asserted in three several memorials presented to His Majesty in May, 1699, by the Lord President and Lord Advocate, on behalf of the company of Scotland, trading to Africa and the Indies. 8° n.p. 1700.

200 Proclamation for apprehending Captains Gavine Hamilton, Kenneth Mackenzie, and Kenneth Urquhart [25th July, 1700].

201 The application of the Scots to foreign trade, commended and encouraged: and their late attempt to have settled Darien, fully vindicated from all that hath been excepted against it. 8° 1700.

202 Caledonia; or the pedlar turned merchant. A tragi-comedy, as it was acted by His Majesty's subjects of Scotland, in the King of Spain's Province of Darien. 4° London 1700.

203 Proclamation for apprehending Walter Herries. Fol. 1701.

204 Hamilton, John, Lord Belhaven. A speech . . . on the affairs of the Indian and African Company, and its Colony of Caledonia. 4° [? Edinburgh] 1701.

205 [? Herries or Harris, Walter.] An inquiry into the Caledonian project, with a defence of England's procedure (in point of equity) in relation thereunto. 4° London 1701.

207 [Paterson, William.] A proposal to plant a colony in Darien; to protect the Indians against Spain and to open the trade of South America to all nations.

(Written in 1701, printed by S. Bannister in *The Writings of William Paterson* in 1857.)

208 A new Darien artifice laid open; in a notable instance of Captain Maclean's name being used (in *The Flying Post*, February 11 and 13, 1709-10) to vouch for the Caledonian Company, after that gentleman hath been persecuted by them these thirteen months past for vouching against them. Authore anti Dariensi. 4° London 1701.

209 Her Majesties most gracious letter to the Parliament, in answer to the address from the Parliament in relation to the company. Fol. Edinburgh 1702.

210 London, the 27th of April, 1702—Saturday last the following address of the Council-General of the . . . company was presented to Her Majesty.

211 Byres, James. A letter to a friend at Edinburgh from Roterdam; giving an account of the Scots affair in Darien. 8° n.p. 1702.

212 The petition of the court of directors of the company . . . 11th August, 1704. The case of the company . . . with relation to their two ships, the "Speedwell" and the "Annandale," with their respective cargo's. Fol. n.p. [1704.]

213 Information for Mr. Alexander Higgins, procurator-fiscal for the High Court of Admiralty, against Captain Thomas Green, commander of the "Worcester," and his crew and complices. Fol. [1705.]

214 Information for Captain Thomas Green, commander of the "Worcester," Captain John Madden, his chief mate, and others, against Mr. Alexander Higgins, advocate, procurator-fiscal of the High Court of Admiralty. Fol. [1705.]

215 A true and impartial account of the proceedings against Capt. Green and his crew, together with the confessions of severals of them under sentence of death. Fol. [1705.]

(The trial is reported in Howell's *State Trials*, 1812, xiv.)

216 The case of Capt. Tho. Green, commander of the ship "Worcester," and his crew, tried and condemned for piracy and murder, in the High Court of Admiralty of Scotland. 4° London 1705.

217 The tryal of Captain Thomas Green, and his crew, pursued before the judge of the High Court of Admiralty of Scotland. Fol. Edinburgh 1705.

218 The petition of the Scots East India and African Company, for reprisal of the ship "Worcester"(Tho. Green, commander) from East India, now seized in Scotland by the said company, for reprisal of the ship "Annandale," seized in England, by the English East India Company. Fol. London 1705.

219 A letter from Scotland to a friend in London; containing a particular narrative of the whole proceedings against the "Worcester" and her crew, from her first arrival in Leith Roads to the 20th of April, 1705. 4° London 1705.

220 The conditions and articles of the intended roup of the ship "Worcester," lying in Bruntisland harbour, and of her cargo lying in ware-houses in Leith. Fol. 1705.

221 Madagascar, or Robert Dury's journal during fifteen years' captivity on that island, written by himself, digested into order, and now published at the request of his friends. London 1729. Reprinted 1890.

(According to this account the captain of the "Speedwell," for whose murder Green was executed, was alive in Madagascar after 1705.)

222 Hamilton, Alexander. New account of the East Indies. London 1727.

(Gives evidence of an act of piracy by Green prior to 1703—*c.f. Historical Mysteries*, by Andrew Lang, pp. 190-213.)

223 [Taylor, Joseph.] A journey to Edenborough in Scotland [in 1705], with notes by William Cowan. 4° Edinburgh 1903.

(Contains descriptions of the trial and execution of Green.)

224 The humble representation of the Council-General of the Company [27th November, 1706]. Fol. 1706.

225 A full and exact account of the proceedings of the court of directors and Council-General of the company . . . with relation to the Treaty of Union, now under the Parliament's consideration. In a letter to a person of quality.
4° 1706.

226 Overture for an act concerning the payment of the sums out of the equivalent to the African Company. Fol. [1706.]

227 [Letter to the members of the Council-General. Edinburgh, 3rd February, 1707.] Fol.

228 Report of the committee concerning the Indian and African Company, Edinburgh, 21st February, 1707. Fol.
(Reprinted in Defoe's *History of the Union.*)

229 Overture concerning the debts of the African and Indian Company. Fol. [1707.]
(Reprinted in Defoe's *History of the Union*—Appendix.)

230 S. R. [? Seton, Robert.] Some neutral considerations with relation to two printed papers, which are cry'd about the streets, viz., *The Committee of Parliament's Report concerning the Indian and African Company*, and *An Overture concerning the Debts of the said Company* [Nos. 228, 229].
Fol. [1707.]

231 Proclamation anent payment to the proprietors of the African Company [21st August, 1707]. Fol.

232 To the . . . Privy Council. The directors of the late Company of Scotland trading to Africa and the Indies [18th September, 1707]. Fol.

233 The case of the late Indian and African Company of Scotland with other part owners of the ships "Speedwell" and "Annandale."
Fol. [1707.]

234 The humble petition of William Paterson, Esq.
Fol. [? 1707-8.]

235 Reports and extracts out of the register books of the African and Indian Company, relating to Mr. Paterson's claim on the said company. Fol. [1708.]

236 The case of Mr. William Paterson, in relation to his claim on the equivalent, as the same is stated in a petition given in by himself, and a report made by Mr. Roderick Mackenzie to the Honourable Court of Exchequer in North Britain.
Fol. [1708.]

237 Reasons against the relief of William Paterson.
Fol. ? 1710.

238 [Borland, Rev. Francis.] Memoirs of Darien, giving a short description of that countrey, with an account of the attempts of the company of Scotland to settle a colonie in that place. With a relation of some of the many tragical disasters that did attend that design. Written mostly in the year 1700, while the author was in the American regions.
8° Glasgow 1714.

(Reprinted Glasgow, 1779.)

239 Report of a Committee of the House of Commons upon the petition of William Paterson [23rd May, 1715].
8° 1715.

(Paterson was finally awarded £18,241 10s. 10$\frac{2}{3}$d.—*c.f. Journals of the House of Commons*, xvii., p. 461; *A History of William Paterson*, by J. S. Barbour, pp. 193, 222-6.)

Note.—Several of the tracts noted below also contain references to the Darien Company, *e.g.*, Nos. 240, 242, 260, 308, 322.

THE MODERN PERIOD, 1696 TO 1707.

The failure of the Darien Company, together with other causes, produced a remarkable depression in trade in Scotland. Distress amongst all classes was very great, and many schemes were propounded with a view to effecting a remedy. The currency was in a bad state, and the difficulties of the nation were felt to consist in "a want of money." Therefore efforts were directed towards the devising of schemes to increase the circulating medium. One group of these consisted in proposals for a further debasement of the coinage; while another, in which John Law, Dr. Hugh Chamberlain, and Dr. Andrew Brown participated, aimed in various ways at establishing an inconvertible paper currency. While many proposals of the latter type had an appearance of plausibility to a country in deep distress, it was inevitable that the expression of so many diverse views as to the management of the currency (Nos. 240-4, 250, 260-3, 265, 267, 272, 273, 278, 285, 286-290, 296, 298, 300-302, 304-306, 308, 310, 338)* would have the effect of forcing thoughtful people towards some understanding of the nature and functions of money. While the prevailing presuppositions of the time led to confusion of money with wealth, there are signs that a few saw deeper than this. Even as early as 1695 the Earl of Cromarty had shown (No. 134) money was nothing more than "a common standard to procure any kind of goods" and he characterises the prohibition of the export of bullion as "folly." In practical life the influence of John Holland, and perhaps that of Paterson, sufficed to prevent any of the projects for an inconvertible paper currency from being adopted.

Closely connected with this period of distress were schemes for curtailing what was described as "excessive luxury" (Nos. 252, 264, 266), and also for the relief of the poor (Nos. 244, 253, 264, 273, 314, 318). The existing system, which Fletcher of Saltoun

* These papers bear evidence of having been drawn up for submission to the Government or to Parliament. Only those have been noted which are at libraries. The list could be considerably extended by a reference to the series of Parliamentary Papers at the Register House, which contains many additional printed memorials and even some pamphlets.

condemned, is said to have cost £150,000 a year, and most suggestions involved the continuance of forced labour. "Hospitals" or workhouses had been tried, but it appears the experiment at Edinburgh had not been a success, since the inmates "escaped" and begged in the streets.

Meanwhile agriculture remained backward, and it is interesting to note the appearance of a small tract on this subject by James Donaldson in 1696 (Nos. 245, 251), in which fallowing and rotation of crops are recommended. The author, however, had reason to complain of the reception given to his book (No. 272). A short tract on mines (No. 294) and a series of tracts on the finances of Glasgow (Nos. 256-8) are also of interest.

Besides the topics already mentioned, a considerable amount of attention was given to trade, manufactures, and fishing, more especially in relation to the Union with England (Nos. 268-9, 271, 274, 276, 279-284, 291-3, 295-6, 299, 300, 303, 304, 307, 309, 311, 314, 320-337, 340-344).

Note.—Nos. 2-5, 10, 15, 24, 26, 30, 35, 39, 44, 46, 50, 59, 64, 79, 106, 109 extend into this period.

---

240 Some account of the transactions of Mr. William Paterson, in relation to the Bank of England and the Orphans' Fund. In a letter to a friend. With the addition of a preface by R. M. relative to a late scandalous pamphlet concerning the Indian and African Company and the Bank of Scotland.
Fol. Edinburgh 1696.

241 Holland, John. A short discourse on the present temper of the nation with respect to the Indian and African Company, and of the Bank of Scotland. Also of Mr. Paterson's pretended Fund of Credit. 4° Edinburgh 1696.

242 A letter to a member of Parliament concerning the Bank of Scotland and the lowering of interest of money.
4° Edinburgh 1696.

243 Old Scots Bank Notes [with reproductions 1696-1804].
(*The Scottish Antiquary*, xi., xii., xiii. ; *A Century of Banking in Dundee*, by C. W. Boase, 1867 ; *The One Pound Note*, by W. Graham, 1886.)

244 [? A(rmour), J.] A proposal to supply the defect of money and relief to the poor. [? Edinburgh 1696.]

245 Donaldson, James. Husbandry anatomised, or an inquiry into the present manner of teiling and manuring the ground in Scotland for most part. 12° Edinburgh 1696.

246 Commission for examining witnesses anent the importation of Irish victual. 4th February, 1696.
s. sh. [Edinburgh 1696.]

247 List of pollable persons within the shire of Aberdeen, 1696.
(Printed by the Spalding Club, 1844.)

248 Cary, John. A discourse concerning the trade of Ireland and Scotland as they stand in competition with the trade of England, being taken out of *An Essay on Trade.*
4° Bristol. Reprinted London 1696.

249 Heriot, Alexander. A book containing tables for finding out the exchange of money and annual rents. 4° 1697.

250 Overture for establishing a society to improve the kingdom.
4° [? Edinburgh 1698.]

251 Donaldson, James. Postscript to *Husbandry anatomiz'd.*
8° [Edinburgh] 1698.

252 Proposal of an Act to be past, for restraining the expenses of apparel. s. sh. [? Edinburgh 1698.]

253 Fletcher, Andrew, of Saltoun. Two discourses concerning the affairs of Scotland. 8° Edinburgh 1698.

254 Act of the Town Council of Edinburgh [13th December, 1699] anent women-servants in taverns. s. sh. [Edinburgh 1699.]

255 The experienced market-man and woman: or profitable instructions how to know the goodness of all sorts of provisions and prevent being cheated. 8° Edinburgh 1699.

256 A letter from —— to his friend, concerning the state of the town of Glasgow's business. 4° [? Glasgow 1699.]

257 B. J. A letter from a citizen of Glasgow to his friend at Edinburgh. Containing some modest animadversions on a late printed letter, concerning the affairs of that city.
4° [? Glasgow] 1700.

258 Reflexions on two late letters concerning the affairs of the City of Glasgow. 4° n.p. 1700.

259 [Seton, Sir William, of Pitmedden.] A short speech prepared to be spoken, by a worthy member in Parliament, concerning the present state of the nation. 8° 1700.

260 [Fletcher, Andrew, of Saltoun.] Overtures offered to the Parliament, in which this proposition is advanced, that a small summ imposed on the nation, for reforming our standard, and for repairing the losses of the African and Indian Company, etc., bestow'd in the method propos'd will be ten times more value to the nation in general, etc., to almost the whole individual persons in the kingdom, than the same summ will be if retained in each particular hand.
4° Edinburgh 1700.

262 Chamberlain, Hugh. A few proposals humbly recommending to the serious consideration of His Majesty's High Commissioner, and the Rt. Hon. the Estates of Parliament, the establishing of a land-credit in this kingdom; with several explanations of, and arguments for, the same; together with full arguments to all such objections as have hitherto appeared against it.
4° Edinburgh 1700.

263 Chamberlain, Hugh. Proposal by Dr. H. Chamberlain and James Armour, for a land-credit. Fol. n.p. n.d.

264 A letter to a member of Parliament occasioned by the growing poverty of the nation from the want and decay of trade, and wrong management thereof. With some overtures for increasing and promoting the one and rectifying the other.
4° Edinburgh 1700.

265 Several particulars of the highest concern to the Kingdom of Scotland, offered to consideration, in order to the enriching the same; without interfering with, or meanly depending on foreign nations. 4° Edinburgh 1700.

266 A proposal for remeeding our excessive luxury.
4° [? Edinburgh 1700.]

267 Overtures offered to the Parliament for reforming our standard.
Edinburgh 1700.

268 A speech without doors concerning the exportation of wool.
4° [? Edinburgh 1700.]

269 General heads and questions touching the manufactories and fisheries of Scotland, submitted to all such as have an interest therein. Fol. [? Edinburgh 1700.]

270 [Seton, William, jun., of Pitmedden.] The interest of Scotland in three essays, viz., I., of the true, original, and indifferency of Church government; II., of the Union of Scotland and England into one monarchy; III., of the present state of Scotland. 8° Edinburgh 1700.

271 Memorial showing the advantages the Kingdom of Scotland may have by the undertaking and improvement of fishings for export. 4° [? Edinburgh] 1700.

272. Donaldson, James. The undoubted art of thriving; wherein is showed—1, That a million £ sterling money, or more if need be, may be raised for propagating the trade of the nation; 2, how the Indian and African Company may propagat their trade; 3, how every one according to his quality may live comfortably and happily. 12° Edinburgh 1701.

273 [Donaldson, James.] Certain and infallible measures laid down whereby the whole begging poor of the kingdom may be alimented at much less charge than they are at present; and begging entirely suppress'd. 4° Edinburgh 1701.

274 [Paterson, William.] Proposals and reasons for constituting a Council of Trade. Edinburgh 1701.

275 [Morer, Rev. Thomas.] A short account of Scotland, with . . . the expence on the civil and military list. 8° London 1702.

276 Memorial concerning the state of the manufactures before and since the year 1700. Fol. n.p. [? 1702.]

277 Establishment for the pay of Her Majesty's standing forces in the Kingdom of Scotland, 15th May, 1702.
(Printed in *The Miscellany of the Maitland Club*, iii., Part i.)

278 Armour, James, of Glasgow. A promonitor warning; or, advice by a true lover of his country, unto all [into] whose hands this may come. 4° [Edinburgh] 1702.

279 [Ridpath, George.] A discourse upon the Union of Scotland and England. 8° n.p. 1702.

280 [Ridpath, George.] The case of Scotsmen residing in England and in the English plantations. Containing an account of the reasons in law why they look upon themselves as entituled to all the priviledges of the natives of England. Of the difficulties they labour under, by a new construction of some late Acts of Parliament: with instances under that head. And of their reasons why they think they are not excluded from the priviledges of Englishmen by those Acts: and that it is not to the interest of England they should be so.
4° Edinburgh (reprinted) 1703.

281 [Brown, Andrew, M.D., of Dolphinton.] Some very weighty and seasonable considerations tending to dispose, excite, and qualify the nation for the more effectual treating with England in relation to an union of confederacy, as the nearest and most proper expedient to put the nation in a way of prosperitie and thriving. 4° n.p. 1703.

282 Several grievances given by a country man anent decay of trade within the Kingdom of Scotland. s. sh. n.p. [1703.]

283 A short proposal anent the export of wool. s. sh. n.p. 1704.

284 A letter from a gentleman in the city to his friend in the country.
4° [1704.]

285 A proposition for remeding the debasement of coyne in Scotland.

286 A further proposal relating to the coyne. n.p. n.d.

287 A further explication of the proposal relating to the coyne.
n.p. n.d.

288 A letter to a member of Parliament from a wel-wisher of his country, in relation to coin. 4° n.p. [1704.]

289 The crying down of the money considered.
Fol. [Edinburgh] 1704.

290 Memorial and intimation from the Governour and Company of the Bank of Scotland, concerning the present state thereof, 28 Dec., 1704. s. sh. n.p. n.d.

(Reprinted in *A Century of Banking in Dundee*, by C. W. Boase, 1867.)

291 A letter to a member of Parliament concerning manufacture and trade. 4° [Edinburgh] 1704.

292 An essay concerning inland and foreign, publick and private trade; together with some overtures, shewing how a company or national trade may be constituted in Scotland, with the advantages which will result therefrom. 4° n.p. [1704.]

293 [Fletcher, Andrew, of Saltoun.] Scotland's interest; or, the great benefit and necessity of a communication of trade with England. Being a brief account of the chief motives that ought to engage us to insist on it at this juncture: and of the great danger of neglecting to do so. Humbly offered to the consideration of the High Court of Parliament. 4° n.p. 1704.

294 [Binning, John.] A letter [on mines] to a member of Parliament. 4° [Edinburgh 1704.]

295 The occasion of Scotland's decay in trade, with a proper expedient for the recovery thereof, and the increase of our wealth. 4° n.p. 1705.

296 The circumstances of Scotland consider'd, with reference to the present scarcity of money, together with some proposals for supplying the defect thereof and rectifying the ballance of trade. 4° [Edinburgh] 1705.

298 [Donaldson, James.] Money encreas'd, and credit rais'd; a proposal for multiplying the tale of money, by coining a certain quantity of lye-money out of a third-part of the plate of the kingdom whereupon a national bank may be erected to the increase of money and trade. 4° Edinburgh 1705.

299 [Ridpath, George.] The reducing of Scotland by arms, and annexing it to England as a province considered. With an historical account of the grievances the Scots complain they have suffer'd in their religion, liberty, and trade since the Union of the Crowns. 4° London, reprinted Edinburgh 1705.

300 [Seton, Sir William.] Some thoughts on ways and means for making this nation a gainer in foreign commerce; and for supplying the present scarcity of money. 8° Edinburgh 1705.

301 Two overtures. . . . 1, For supplying the present scarcity of coyn and improving trade; 2, for clearing the debts due by the Government to the army and the civil list. 4° 1705.

302 A present remedie for the want of money; or, some remarks upon a paper, intituled, *An Overture for Supplying the Present Scarcity of Money*, etc. [No. 301]. 4° [? 1705.]

303 Several matters relating to the improvement of the trade of this kingdom. n.d.

304 An essay for promoting of trade, and increasing the coin of the nation. In a letter from a gentleman in the country to his friend at Edinburgh, a member of Parliament.
4° n.p. [1705.]

305 [Law, John, of Lauriston.] Money and trade considered, with a proposal for supplying the nation with money.
4° Edinburgh 1705.

306 [Brown, Andrew, M.D.] An essay on the new project for a land-mint, proposing a proper and practical scheme and expedient and how to put the same under due and regular management, not only for the speedy supplying of money; but also for the advancing of trade and other national improvements. By the author of *The Character of the True Public Spirit*. 8° Edinburgh 1705.

307. A scheme of Scotland's product and manufactures, by which we may ballance with any port or nation, needful for us, beside other priviledges and advantages we enjoy.
4° n.p. [1705.]

308 Hodges, James. Considerations and proposals for supplying the present scarcity of money and advancing trade.
4° Edinburgh 1705.

309 S[preul] J[ohn]. An accompt current betwixt Scotland and England balanced; together with an essay or a scheme of the product of Scotland, as also a view of the several products of the ports or nations we trade to.
4° Edinburgh 1705.

(Reprinted 1882.)

310 Proposals by Dr. Hugh Chamberlen and James Armour for a land credit. Fol. 1705.

311 To his Grace, Her Majesties High Commissioner, an te Honorable Estates of Parlment. Te address far te fishers on te Highland coasts, an all uthers inhapiting te Highlands, wha it ma concern, humbly representing tat it will be disadvantageous to Her nane sel, tat te Articles of te Union concerning salt and excise pe agreed to, without an mendment in case the Union is concluded. 4° [? Edinburgh ? 1705.]
(Reprinted in *The Scottish Antiquary*, xii.)

312 To his grace Her Majesties High Commissionir and the Honourable Estates of Parliament. The humble petition of the per shank workers and finger spinners of Aberdeen, and the places thereabout.
(Reprinted in *The Scottish Antiquary*, xii.)

313 Forbes, William. A treatise of Church lands and tithes, in two parts. 12° Edinburgh 1705.

314 [Seton, William, jun., of Pitmedden.] Scotland's great advantages by an Union with England: showen in a letter from the country to a member of Parliament. 4° n.p. 1706.
(Reprinted in *Somers' Tracts.*)

315 A letter concerning the consequence of an incorporating Union, in relation to trade. 4° 1706.

316 An essay upon the Union of the Kingdoms of England and Scotland. [? 1706.]
(Printed in *Somers' Tracts.*)

317 [Black, David.] Essay upon industry and trade, shewing the necessity of the one, the conveniency and usefulness of the other, and the advantages of both. 4° Edinburgh 1706.

318 The petition of the begging and wanting poor in the nation. Fol. n.p. [? 1706.]

319 A copy of a letter from a country farmer to his laird. [1706.]
(Reprinted in *The Scottish Antiquary*, xii.)

321 Answer to a letter concerning trade, sent from several Scots gentlemen that are merchants in England, to their countrymen that are merchants in Scotland. 4° Edinburgh 1706.

322 Some considerations in relation to trade, humbly offered to his Grace, her Majesty's high commissioner, and the Estates of Parliament. 4° Edinburgh 1706.

323 [Donaldson, James.] *Considerations in relation to Trade* considered, and a short view of our present trade and taxes compared with what these taxes may amount to after the Union, reviewed. 4° Edinburgh 1706.

324 [Black, William, advocate.] A short view of our present trade and taxes, compared with what these taxes may amount to after the Union; with some reasons why if we enter into an Union our trade should be under our own regulations. 4° Edinburgh 1706.

325 [Black, William, advocate.] Remarks upon a pamphlet entitled *The Considerations in relation to Trade considered* [No. 323] and *A Short View of our Present Trade and Taxes reviewed* [No. 324]. 4° [? Edinburgh] 1706.

326 The state of the excise, etc., vindicated from the remarks of the author of *The Short View* [No. 324]. 1706.

327 The state of the excise after the Union compared with what it is now. 4° 1706.

328 [Paterson, William.] An inquiry into the reasonableness and consequences of an Union with Scotland. Containing a brief deduction of what hath been done, designed, or proposed in that matter of an Union, during the last age. A scheme of an Union, as accommodated to the present circumstances, of the two nations. Also the states of the respective revenues, debts, weights, measures, taxes and impositions, and of other facts of moment. 8° London 1706.

329 The anatomy of an equivalent, by the Marquess of Halifax [No. 124]. Adapted to the equivalent in the present articles [of the Union]. 4° [Edinburgh 1706.]

330 An essay upon the equivalent in a letter to a friend. 4° 1706.

331 [? Clerk, John.] An essay upon the fifteenth article of the Treaty of Union, wherein the difficulties that arise upon equivalents are fully cleared and explained. 4° 1706.

332 [Defoe, Daniel.] An essay at removing national prejudices against a Union with England.

Part I. 4° London 1706.
Part II. 4° London 1706.
Part III. 4° [Edinburgh] 1706.
A Fourth Essay. 4° Edinburgh 1706.
A Fifth Essay. 4° [? Edinburgh] 1707.
Two great questions considered : being the Sixth Essay.
4° [? Edinburgh] 1707.

333 [Black, William, advocate.] A letter concerning *The Remarks upon the Considerations of Trade* [No. 325], by the author of the *Fourth Essay at Removing National Prejudices.*
4° n.p. ? 1706.

334 [Black, William, advocate.] Some overtures and cautions in relation to trade and taxes, humbly offered to the Parliament.
4° n.p. 1707.

335 A letter concerning the Union, with relation to trade. From several Scots gentlemen, merchands in England, to their country-men, merchants in Scotland. 8° London 1707.

336 Some overtures and cautions in relation to trade and taxes, humbly offered to Parliament. 4° n.p. 1707.

337 Remarks for the salt-masters, fishers of salmond . . . and others who make use of Scots salt, humbly offered upon the eighth article of the Treaty of Union.
s. sh. Fol. [? 1707.]

338 The crying down of the money considered.
Fol. [Edinburgh] 1707.

339 Acts of the Royal Burghs of Scotland [from returns made in 1708].
(Printed by the Scottish Burgh Records Society—*Miscellany*, 1881.)

340 A letter from a Scots factor at London to a merchant in Edinburgh, concerning the proceeding of the House of Commons; to prevent the importation of wine and other goods from Scotland. London, 17 April, 1707.

341 Reasons against passing the bill to prevent carrying foreign goods from Scotland to England, after the Union, contained in a second letter from a Scots factor at London to a merchant at Edinburgh. s. sh. [? Edinburgh 1707.]

342 Stewart, Walter, and Murray, William. Observations on the Acts made for the encouragement of the Lustrings Company, which relate to the exportation of French a-la-modes and lustrings. s. sh. n.p. [? 1707-8.]

343 The trade of Britain stated, being the substance of two papers published in London, on occasion of the importation of wine and brandy from North Britain. [1708.]

344 Defoe, Daniel. The history of the Union between England and Scotland, with a collection of original papers relating thereto. Fol. Edinburgh 1709.

(Contains many documents relating to Scottish coinage, customs and excise, revenue, trade, and the Darien Company.)

THE MODERN PERIOD TO 1776.

THE period from the Union to the appearance of the *Wealth of Nations* may be conveniently dealt with as one whole, and it is possessed of peculiar interest as showing the material that was available for Adam Smith in his own country. Considering this period of over seventy years from the standpoint of general industrial progress, it must be remembered that the Union involved considerable commercial adjustment, and that for some time Scotland continued poor. For instance, to take only one industry to which great attention was paid, namely the linen trade, the quantity stamped for sale in 1728 was only 2,183,977½ yards, increasing by 1743 to 5,061,311 yards, and by 1766 to 13,224,557 yards (Nos. 427, 435). Much attention was given to this trade (Nos. 365-70, 405, 410, 415, 432, 477, 501, 520, 525, 528), also to fishing (Nos. 347, 349, 357, 372, 378-9, 389, 390, 392-3, 405, 415, 423, 436, 446, 447), and particularly to agriculture (Nos. 345, 346, 381, 388, 402, 403, 405, 426, 434, 447, 459, 469, 470, 478, 486, 500, 509, 521, 526, 540). The anxiety for the improvement of the land was a slower, but ultimately a much more satisfactory, means of increasing the national wealth than the doubtful schemes that had been proposed just before the Union. In this movement the names of Campbell and Dickson are of importance, chiefly in relation to the controversy between large and small farms and in inquiring into the causes of the movements in prices of provisions. Closely connected with agriculture were the efforts of a body known as the York Buildings Company (Nos. 360-3, 371, 382-7, 406-8, 411-13), which was in reality a land-development concern, and which aimed at exploiting forfeited estates it had purchased.* Then in quite a different connection the problems of land-tenure and entails were important (Nos. 356, 375, 404, 440-1, 464, 487, 497, 498-9). Questions

* For an account of the York Buildings Company *vide The York Buildings Company*, by D. Murray, Glasgow, 1883; *The Constitution and Finance of English, Scottish, and Irish Joint-Stock Companies to 1720*, by W. R. Scott, Cambridge, 1911, iii., pp. 418-434.

concerning banking, paper money, and credit were from time to time forced on the attention of observers of the tendencies of their time; and, partly by sad experience, partly by the knowledge gained through these inquiries, Scotland was in advance of England on this point, so that the former escaped the great losses through failure of banks which happened in the first quarter of the nineteenth century (Nos. 355, 377, 380, 395-6, 398, 420, 421, 424, 454, 460, 462, 465, 472-6, 488-96A, 510, 521, 529). Attention may be drawn to works relating to foreign trade and the staple (Nos. 350-1, 444, 507, 539), to manufactures (Nos. 425, 436, 438, 463, 531), to the cloth trade (Nos. 439, 463, 525, 528, 535), to brewing and distilling (Nos. 433, 442). Problems of charity continue to obtain notice (Nos. 373, 394, 397, 400-1, 405, 419, 422, 426, 452, 466, 468, 471, 523-4, 537-8), while the relation of the municipality to the traders of the town will be found illustrated in Nos. 376, 416, 417, 430-1, 457, 458, 482-5, 533-4. The general progress of the country is shown by a series of tracts relating to the stipends of ministers, as well as in some other pamphlets (Nos. 414, 449, 450, 451, 456).

Together with the descriptive treatment of economic phenomena, generally with a view to some practical end, one notes the beginning of a tendency towards a more scientific examination of the questions discussed. This is to be noticed in the case both of metallic and paper money, and the same spirit begins to show itself in the portions of the works of Hutcheson and Hume (Nos. 428 and 461), which treat of economic subjects. Of all the writers in Scotland, Hutcheson is the only one that can be suggested, with any degree of confidence, as having influenced Adam Smith towards the adoption of the principle of division of labour, but a comparison of the two writers on this topic shows the immensely greater width of Adam Smith's treatment. Some Continental writers on the history of economics have advanced claims on behalf of Sir James Steuart (whose *Inquiry into the Principles of Political Economy* appeared in 1767) as the founder of the scientific treatment of the subject. No doubt Steuart has the spirit of a scientific investigator, but his treatment of the problems he investigates tends to be eclectic, and it certainly wants the constructive ability and charm of style that one finds in Adam Smith. At the same time, it is not to be assumed that the causes of the appearance of the *Wealth of Nations* are to be assigned wholly to Smith himself. The widespread interest in economic questions in Scotland for thirty years before the book was published must have been fruitful, not only in stimulating discussion, but also in collecting a considerable amount of material which Smith was able to use to advantage.

Note.—Nos. 4, 5, 11, 24, 26, 30, 35, 39, 44, 46, 50, 59, 79, and 106 extend into this period.

---

345 A dissertation on the chief obstacles to the improvement of land.
8° Aberdeen 1709.

346 An expedient from preventing the dearth of victual, humbly offered to the consideration of the honourable justices of the peace, the gentlemen heritors, etc., met at the Quarter Sessions at Edinburgh, May 14, 1709.
s. sh. Edinburgh 1709.

347 The case of several merchants and others, concerned in the fishery of North Britain. Fol. s. sh. [London] 1711.

348 A description of the most remarkable highways, and well-known fairs and mercats in Scotland, with several other remarkable things. 12° Edinburgh 1711.

349 Proposal for improving the fishery of Great Britain.
4° London 1713.

350 The eighth and ninth articles of the treaty of commerce, with relation to the trade of Scotland with France considered.
8° Edinburgh 1713.

351 The trade of Scotland with France considered, in two letters directed to the author of *Mercator*. 4° Edinburgh 1713.

352 Edgar, William. Vestigalium Systema, or a complete view of that part of the revenue of Great Britain, commonly called Customs. 8° London 1714.
(Contains a list of Scottish Ports.)

353 The original design, progress, and present state of the Scots corporation at London, of the foundation of King Charles II.
4° London 1714.

354 Accompt of expenses in Edinburgh by Alexander Rose of Kilravock, 1715.
(Printed in *Miscellany* of the Scottish History Society, i.)

355 Holland, John. The ruine of the Bank of England and all publick credit inevitable, and the necessity, in a short time, of stopping the payments upon the several funds of the Bank, South Sea Company, lotteries, &c., if the honourable House of Commons will not themselves be judges of the means that may be offer'd to prevent it. 4° [London] 1715.

356 [Hepburn of Bairford.] A discourse concerning feus and superiorities, shewing that the rigid observance of them is inconsistent with the nature of the British constitution. Humbly address'd to the Parliament of Great Britain. 8° Edinburgh 1716.

357 Reasons for taking off the present prohibition of curing fish in Scotland, with British salt, for exportation; while the English lie under no such restraint. s. sh. n.p. [1717.]

358 [Paterson, William.] An inquiry into the state of the Union of Great Britain and the past and present state of the trade and public revenues thereof. London 1717.

(Reprinted by S. Bannister in *The Writings of William Paterson.*)

359 Forbes, William. A methodical treatise concerning bills of exchange; with cases relating to the law of Scotland, and views of the laws and customs of England and other countries. 12° Edinburgh 1718.

360 [Dalrymple, David, Lord Hailes.] Observations on the bill for the sale of the forfeited estates; with reasons against it, humbly offered to the consideration of both Houses of Parliament. 8° Edinburgh 1718.

361 [Haldane, Patrick.] The case of the forfeited estates in Scotland, consider'd, in a letter to a noble L——d. 8° Edinburgh 1718.

362 The laws and judicatures of Scotland vindicated from the calumnies contained in a late pamphlet, intituled, *The Case of the Forfeited Estates in Scotland consider'd, in a letter to a noble L——d* [No. 361]. 8° London 1718.

363 Letter . . . concerning the proceedings of the commissioners and trustees for the forfeitures in Scotland. 1720.

364 [Dalrymple, Sir David.] Time bargains tried by the rules of equity, and principles of the civil law. 8° London (reprinted Edinburgh) 1720.

365 The case of the printing of linnens in Great Britain as it particularly relates to the printing of linnens made in Scotland. Fol. [? 1720.]

366 Reasons for encouraging the linen manufactories in North Britain. s. sh. Fol. [? London ? 1720.]

367 The case of the printed linnens of North Britain [with reference to a bill in Parliament to retain the use of printed and painted calicoes]. Fol. s. sh. [? London 1720.]

368 The true case of the Scots linnen manufacture, humbly offered to the consideration of the honourable House of Commons. s. sh. Fol. London ? 1720.

369 The answer of the Scots linnen manufacturers to the report of the Lords Commissioners of Trade and Plantations; and to a paper falsely called *The Case of the Printing of Linnen in Great Britain*, etc., humbly submitted to the consideration of the hon. House of Commons. s. sh. Fol. London. ? 1720.

370 The Scots linen manufacturers answer to two papers, intituled, *The Case of the woollen and silk Manufacturers of Great Britain* and *The Case of the Printed Linnens in Great Britain*. s. sh. [London ? 1720.]

371 Extracts from two acts of Parliament, relating to the Governour and Company of Undertakers for raising the Thames water in York Buildings. s. sh. Fol. [London 1720.]

372 Articles of the Co-partnery of the Freemen Burgesses of the Royal Burrows of Scotland, for carrying on a fishing trade, dated at Edinburgh, 8, 9, 10, 11, 12 August, 1720. 8° Edinburgh 1720.

373 Some of the grievances and complaints of the poor commonalty of Scotland. 8° Glasgow 1720.

374 The cry of the creditors upon bankrupt estates in Scotland renewed; containing a project for retrieving credit, and advancing trade by preventing tedious law-suits. 8° Edinburgh 1721.

375 [Logan, William, of Logan.] A letter to an English member of Parliament, from a gentleman in Scotland, concerning the slavish dependencies, which a great part of that nation is still kept under, by superiorities, wards, reliefs and other remains of the feudal law and by clanships and tithes. 8° Edinburgh 1721.

376 A vindication of the conduct of the magistrates and town council of Edinburgh, in answer to a Memorial lately published, intituled *Memorial for several Merchants, Burgesses, etc., of the good town of Edinburgh,* against the magistrates of the said city November 29, 1721. Fol. [Edinburgh 1721.]

377 Armour, James. Proposals for making the Bank of Scotland more useful and profitable; and for raising the value of the land interest in North Britain. 4° Edinburgh 1723.

378 A letter from a gentleman in town, to a friend in the country, concerning the present state of the fishing co-partnery in North Britain. 4° Edinburgh 1722.

379 A second letter from a gentleman in town to his friend in the country, about the fishing co-partnery in North Britain. 4° Edinburgh 1724.

380 Holland, John. Some letters relating to the Bank of Scotland . . . published with explanatory remarks, in a letter to the proprietors by R. Holland, M.D. 8° Edinburgh 1723.

381 A treatise concerning the manner of fallowing of ground &c. by the Society for improving in the knowledge of Agriculture. 8° Edinburgh 1724.

382 The case of the York Buildings company. s. sh. Fol. [London 1725.]

383 The Governor and Company for raising Thames water in York Buildings, appellants. J. Haldane . . . respondent. The appellants' case. Fol. [London 1725.]

384 The Governor and Company of Undertakers for raising Thames water in York Buildings, appellants. J. Haldane . . . respondent. The respondent's case. Fol. [London 1725.]

385 Proposals for employing the remaining stock of the fishery, so as to be of universal use and advantage to the nation, in a letter from a gentleman in the country to his friend at Edinburgh. 8° Edinburgh 1725.

386 [Forbes, Duncan, of Culloden.] Copy of a letter from a gentleman in Edinburgh, to his friend in the country upon the subject of a malt tax. 8° [? Edinburgh] 1725.

387 14 March, 1727. Information for the governour and directors of the Company of Undertakers for raising the Thames water in York Buildings . . . against T. Mathie.
Fol. [Edinburgh 1727.]

388 Account of the Glasgow Highland Society, 1727-58.
(*Scots Magazine*, xxiv.)

389 Plan of the commissioners and trustees for improving fisheries and manufactures in Scotland for the application of their funds.
8° Edinburgh 1727.

390 Reasons for improving the fisheries, and the linnen manufacture of Scotland. Wherein are shewn the advantages that must accrue to England by the increase of the Scots linnen manufacture. That the fishing in deep water is equally an advantage to all the subjects of Great Britain. And that England and Scotland are now so closely united in point of interest that severally they must be directly affected in profit and loss by the prosperity and sufferings of each other.
8° London 1727.

391 Letters of John Cockburn of Ormistoun to his gardener, 1727-44.
(Printed by the Scottish History Society, 1904.)

392 An abstract of his Majestie's patent for improving fisheries and manufactures in Scotland. 8° Edinburgh 1727.

393 His Majesty's patent for improving fisheries and manufactures in Scotland. 8° Edinburgh 1728.

394 Gairdner, Andrew. An historical account of the Old People's Hospital, commonly called the Trinity Hospital in Edinburgh; also proposals how to raise a fund for the maintenance of widows and orphans under the title of a Charity Bank.
8° Edinburgh 1728.

395 An historical account of the establishment, progress, and state of the Bank of Scotland; and of the several attempts that have been made against it, and the several interruptions and inconveniences the company has encountered.
4° Edinburgh 1728.

396 A letter containing remarks on *The Historical Account of the Old Bank* [No. 395]. 4° Edinburgh 1728.

397 The case of the poor consider'd. Fol. n.p. 1729.

398 Warrant of the charter erecting the Royal Bank of Scotland.
8° Edinburgh 1729.

399 [Macintosh, Borland.] An essay on ways and means for inclosing, fallowing, planting, etc., Scotland; and that in sixteen years at farthest. 8° Edinburgh 1729.

400 An account of the great advantages of erecting a charitable house for maintaining and employing the poor of this city.
Fol. [Glasgow 1731.]

401 An account of the design of erecting a charity school or workhouse in Glasgow; with proposals thereanent.
Fol. n.p. [1731.]

402 A short enquiry into cause of the general non-improvement of land in Scotland; and the best method to remove it.
8° Edinburgh 1731.

403 [MacIntosh, Borland.] Essay on the husbandry of Scotland, with a proposal for the further improvement thereof. By a lover of his country. 8° Edinburgh 1752.

404 Logan, William, of Logan. A review of the present state of Scotland, in regard to the tenures and slavish dependencies of that part of North Britain. 8° London 1733.

405 [Lindsay, Patrick, Lord Provost of Edinburgh.] The interest of Scotland considered, with regard to its police, in employing of the poor, its agriculture, its trade, its manufactures, and fisheries. 12° Edinburgh 1733.

406 A report from the Committee [of the House of Commons] to whom the petition of the proprietors of the stock of the governor and company for raising the Thames water in York Buildings is referred, May 9, 1733. Fol. London 1733.
(Reprinted in *Reports from Committees of the House of Commons*, i.)

407 Proposals offered to the creditors of the York Buildings Company.
s. sh. Fol. [London 1734.]

408 Proposals for the payment of the creditors of the York Buildings Company. s. sh. Fol. [London 1734.]

409 Edinburgh treasurer's account, 1734-5.
(Printed in *The Scottish Antiquary*, xii.)

410 [Lindsay, Patrick.] Reasons for encouraging the linen manufacture of Scotland and other parts of Great Britain. By the author of *The Interest of Scotland Consider'd.*
8° London 1735.

411 September 12, 1735. York Buildings House. A list of the members of the Corporation and Company of Undertakers for raising the Thames water in York Buildings.
Fol. [London 1735.]

412 Answers for the annuitants upon the estates purchased by the York Buildings Company in Scotland, and their trustees and Mr. J. Hamilton, their factor, to the petition and additional petition presented in the name of the said York Building Company. Fol. [London 1736 ?]

413 A report from the Committee [of the House of Commons] relating to the York Buildings Company, 2 May, 1735.
(Reprinted in *Reports from Committees of the House of Commons*, i.)

414 The claims of the clergy to a Divine right of maintenance . . . exemplified in the pretensions and conduct of the present Scotch clergy. 8° London 1736.

415 Plan of the commissioners and trustees for improving fisheries and manufactures in Scotland for the application of the funds under their management for three years from Christmas, 1736. 8° [Edinburgh 1737.]

416 Proposal for retrieving the sinking state of the good town of Edinburgh, humbly offered to its honest burgesses and well-wishers. 8° Edinburgh 1737.

417 A vindication of the managers of the Royal Infirmary of Edinburgh from the aspersions cast upon their conduct by a late pamphlet. 8° Edinburgh 1737.

418 Ochtertyre house booke of accompts 1737-9.
(Printed by the Scottish History Society, 1907.)

419 A summary view of the rise, constitution and present state of the charitable foundation of King Charles the second, commonly called, the Scots Corporation in London; with an alphabetical list of the benefactors. 4° London 1738.

420 Scotiæ numisma: or, ancient Scottish coins: their real and proportional value; with some observations on the prices of provisions in Scotland in ancient times. 1738.
(Printed by the Clarendon Historical Society, 1883.)

421 Anderson, James. Selectus Diplomatum et Numismatum Scotiæ Thesaurus. Fol. Edinburgh 1739.

(The introduction to the above by Thomas Ruddiman was translated and published separately in 1773.)

422 Proposal for erecting an hospital for employing the poor in Edinburgh, 1739.

(*Scots Magazine*, i.)

423 A letter relating to the improvement of our fishery, etc., 1739.

(*Scots Magazine*, i.)

424 Forbes, Sir William, of Pitsligo. Memoirs of a banking-house. [1740-1803.]

(Printed in 1859.)

425 On the neglect of trade and manufactures [1740].

(*Scots Magazine*, ii.)

426 Murray, Sir Alexander, of Stanhope. The true interest of Great Britain, Ireland, and our plantations. . . . To which is added, a new method of husbandry, by greater and lesser canals, in Scotland; also a letter of remonstrance to Philip, Lord Hardwicke, on the miserable state of Scotland. Fol. London 1740.

427 A list of places and offices in Scotland, at the gift and disposal of the Crown [with salaries], 1741.

(Printed in *The Scottish Antiquary*, xii.)

428 Hume, David. Essays Moral and Political. Edinburgh 1742.

(Includes essays on Commerce, Money, Interest, Balance of Trade, Taxes, Public Credit, and Population.)

429 The petition of John Wilson and Gilbert Blair, Barbers in the Canongate, November 8th 1742. [4° Edinburgh 1742.]

430 Answers for the Corporation of Barbers of Edinburgh, pursuers; to the petition of John Wilson and Gilbert Blair, barbers in the Cannongate, defenders, Nov. 18, 1742. 4° [Edinburgh 1742.]

431 Information for the burgh of the Cannongate against the town of Edinburgh, November 26, 1742. 4° [Edinburgh 1742.]

432 The vast advantage of raising flax [1742].

(*Scots Magazine*, iv.)

433 The history of the British distillery [1743].

(*Scots Magazine*, v.)

434 Maxwell, Robert. Transactions of the Society for promoting Agriculture in Scotland; selected by R. Maxwell.
4° Edinburgh 1743.

435 Report from the Committee [of the House of Commons] as to linens, threads, tapes, 11 March, 1744.
(Reprinted in *Reports from Committees of the House of Commons*, ii.)

436 [Forbes, Duncan, of Culloden.] Some considerations on the present state of Scotland; in a letter to the Commissioners for improving fisheries and manufactures. To which is subjoined, a letter from the annual committee of the convention of royal boroughs, to the several boroughs of Scotland, by order of the general convention, for preventing the pernicious practice of smuggling. 8° Edinburgh 1744.

437 The nature of foreign exchanges [1744].
(*Scots Magazine*, vi.)

438 The present state of Scotland consider'd: and its . . . sinking condition charged upon the conduct of the landed gentlemen. Shewing . . . that the only means of relieving their estates . . . is by their joining together to promote home manufacture. 8° Edinburgh 1745.

439 Smith, John, LL.B. Chronicon Rusticum Commerciale; or Memoirs of wool, etc., being a collection of history and argument, concerning the woolen manufacture and woolen trade in general; particularly the rise, progress, improvements, declensions, revolutions and the respective causes thereof . . . as given by a succession of writers.
2 vols. 8° London 1747.

440 [Home, Henry, Lord Kames.] Essays upon several subjects concerning British antiquities, viz., I. Introduction of the feudal law into Scotland. II. Constitution of Parliament. III. Honour, dignity. IV. Succession or descent, with an appendix upon hereditary and indefeasible right. Composed anno 1747.
8° Edinburgh 1747.

441 [M'Dowall, Andrew, Lord Bankton.] An essay upon feudal holdings, superiorities, and hereditary jurisdictions in Scotland; shewing the nature of feudal holdings, superiorities, and jurisdictions with the casualties and forfeitures incident thereto: the errors and gross misrepresentations touching the same, in a late pamphlet entitled, *Superiorities display'd or Scotland's grievance on account of holdings and hereditary jurisdictions, etc.* 8° London 1747.

442 A short view of the prejudice arising both to the country and the revenue, from the imposition on ale and beer granted to the City of Edinburgh and other boroughs in Scotland.
Edinburgh 1748

443 Contract of copartnery of the Edinburgh Whale-fishing Society.
8° [Edinburgh 1749.]

444 [Stuart, Charles.] The staple contract between the Royall Burrows of Scotland and the City of Campvere in Zealand, with the several amplifications, prolongations and ratifications thereof.
8° Edinburgh 1749.

445 [Fea, James.] The general grievances and oppressions of the Isles of Orkney and Shetland, under the following heads:— I. Of the gradual and continued increase of the weights used in these islands, above the true measure and standard of Norway, from whence they are derived. II. Of the tribute-real or old land tax, which is here kept up. . . . III. Of the double tythes here exacted. . . . IV. Of the true rental of these islands, called the King's rental, and the burdensome rental imposed in place of it. . . . V. Of the arbitrary prices kept up in these demense countries, instead of the Exchequer prices. VI. The conclusion, shewing the dreadful effects of so much oppression.
8° Edinburgh 1750.

446 [Campbell, John, LL.D.] An exact account of the greatest white herring fishery in Scotland, carried on yearly in the Island of Zetland by the Dutch only.
8° London 1750.

447 The laird and the farmer. A dialogue upon farming, trade, cookery, and their method of living in Scotland, balanc'd with that of England. 8° London 1750.

448 Statements by the Council of the Free British Fishery [1751-5].
(*Scots Magazine*, xiii. to xvii.)

449 A collection of all the papers published in relation to the scheme for augmenting the stipends of the established clergy of Scotland. 8° Edinburgh 1751.

450 An impartial account of the rise, progress, and nature of the scheme for augmenting the livings of the Scotch clergy.
Edinburgh 1751.

451 Report from a Committee [of the House of Commons] to whom the petitions of the Commissioners from the General Assembly of the Church of Scotland and also the petition of John, Earl of Morton, were referred, 24 May, 1751.
(Reprinted in *Reports from Committees of the House of Commons*, ii.)

452 Letter from a gentleman in Edinburgh to a friend in London, in relation to the proposals for establishing by law an equal and certain fund, for maintenance and support the begging poor, and out-pensioners of the City of Edinburgh.
4° [? Edinburgh 1751.]

453 [Home, Henry, Lord Kames.] Essays on the principles of morality and natural religion. 8° Edinburgh 1751.

454 A letter from a gentleman in Glasgow to his friend in Edinburgh, concerning bank notes and paper credit.
8° n.p. 1752.

455 Hume, David. Political Discourses. 1752.

456 Proposals for carrying on certain public works in the City of Edinburgh. 8° [? Edinburgh 1752.]
(Contains notes of the development of trade in the Edinburgh district since 1692.)

457 Memorial for the Magistrates and Council of Edinburgh.
4° [Edinburgh ? 1752.]

458 [Chalmer, Andrew.] Some observations in relation to the supreme power of Parliament, touching the compelling of folks to part with their private property for the publick good: with a particular view to the proposal now in agitation, for applying to the Parliament to interpose that power for the sake of the projected improvements of the City of Edinburgh. But also proper for the consideration of every man who has any property in Scotland. 4° [Edinburgh 1752.]

459 Campbell, John, LL.D. A full and particular description of the Highlands of Scotland, its situation and produce.
8° London 1752.

460 [Murray, Patrick, Lord Elibank.] Essays on the public debt, on paper money and on frugality. 8° Edinburgh 1753.

461 Hutcheson, Francis. A System of Moral Philosophy.
2 vols. 4° London 1755.
(The earlier form of the theory of Adam Smith (No. 479) shows marked traces of the influence of Hutcheson—*c.f. Francis Hutcheson*, by W. R. Scott, pp. 230-43.)

462 Account of the run on the Glasgow banks, 1756.
(*Scots Magazine*, xviii.)

463 [Maxwell, George Clerk.] Observations on the method of growing wool in Scotland, and proposals for improving the quality of our wool. In two letters to the Commissioners . . . for improving fisheries and manufactures in Scotland.
8° Edinburgh 1756.

464 Dalrymple, John. An essay towards a general history of feudal property in Great Britain. 8° London 1757.

465 Murray, Patrick, Lord Elibank. Thoughts on money, circulation and paper currency. 4° Edinburgh 1758.
(Reprinted in *A Select Collection of Scarce and Valuable Tracts . . . on Paper Currency* . . . 1857; ed., R. A. J. M'Cullough.)

466 State of the charity workhouse at Edinburgh [1758].
(*Scots Magazine*, xx.)

467 A friendly address to the farmers of Scotland.
8° n.p. 1759

468 [Hepburn, Thomas, minister at Birsay.] A letter to a gentleman [George Paton] from his friend in Orkney, concerning the true causes of the poverty of that country.
8° London 1760.

469 A dissertation on the chief obstacles to the improvement of land, and introducing better methods of agriculture throughout Scotland. 8° Aberdeen 1760.

470 [Dickson, Rev. Adam.] A treatise on agriculture.
8° Edinburgh 1762.

471 Regulations for the charity workhouse of the parish of St. Cuthbert's, or West Kirk, May 27, 1762.
4° [Edinburgh 1762.]

472 An impartial essay concerning the nature and use of specie and paper credit in any country; the difficulties which the banks of Scotland at present labour under, owing to the scarcity of specie, and what may be done for preventing the distress thereby like to fall upon this country. Edinburgh 1762.
(Reprinted *Scots Magazine*, xxiv.)

473 Considerations relating to the late order of the two banks established at Edinburgh, by which they have recalled one-fourth of their cash accounts. Edinburgh 1762.

(Reprinted *Scots Magazine*, xxiv.)

474 A letter to J— F— Esq., on the conduct of the banks. With remarks on a late pamphlet entitled *Considerations*, etc. [1762].

(*Scots Magazine*, xxiv.)

475 Thoughts concerning banks and the paper currency of Scotland [1763].

476 Reflections on the paper currency of Scotland [1763].

(*Scots Magazine*, xxv.)

477 The present state of the linen manufacture of Scotland [1763].

(*Scots Magazine*, xxv.)

478 Small farms a public benefit [1763].

(*Scots Magazine*, xxv.)

479 Smith, Adam. Lectures on justice, police, revenue, and arms, delivered in the University of Glasgow.

(Reported by a student in 1763, printed 1896.)

480 Anderson, Adam. An historical and chronological deduction of the origin of commerce, from the earliest accounts to the present time, containing an history of the British Empire. 2 vols. Fol. London 1764.

(Subsequently revised and extended by Coombe and M'Pherson. Pamphlets and Acts of Parliament relating to Scotland are summarised.)

481 Considerations on the Acts of Parliament relative to highways in Scotland, and on the new scheme of a tax in lieu of statute labour. 8° Edinburgh 1764.

482 Copy suspension for James M'Nabb and Alexander Sinclair against the Incorporation of Taylors in Edinburgh. 8° [Edinburgh 1764.]

483 Answers for the Incorporation of Taylors in Edinburgh to the bill of the said suspension, offered by James M'Nabb and Alexander Sinclair. 8° [Edinburgh 1764.]

484 Replies for James M'Nabb and Alexander Sinclair to the above answers for the Incorporation of Taylors in Edinburgh. 8° [Edinburgh 1764.]

485 [Mein, Robert.] The Edinburgh Paradise regained, or the city set at liberty, to propagate and improve her trade and commerce. Being a curious dissertation thereon, and discovery of the disease that obstructs the growth and progress thereof. And an effectual remedy and cure therefor, by redressing and removing her grievances. 8° Edinburgh 1764.

486 [Dickson, Rev. Adam.] Small farms destructive to the country in its present situation, in answer to a letter published in the Scots and Edinburgh magazines of December, 1762. 8° Edinburgh 1764.

487 Dalrymple, John. Considerations upon the policy of entails in Great Britain, occasioned by a scheme to apply for a statute to let the entails of Scotland die out. 8° Edinburgh 1764.

488 Boase, C. W. A century of banking in Dundee; being the annual balance sheets of the Dundee Banking Company from 1764 to 1864. Containing the balance sheets of other banks of the district [also of the Bank of Scotland, 1704 and 1728], and memoranda concerning Scotch and English banking during the period. 8° Edinburgh 1867.

489 Banking as presently practised in Scotland [1764].

490 A defence of our banks and bankers [1764].

491 A remedy for the present scarcity of silver [1764].

492 The banks and currency of Scotland [1764].

493 Of abolishing or regulating private banking [1764].

494 Resolutions of Aberdeen and Inverness relating to bank notes [1764].

(Nos. 489-494 in *Scots Magazine*, xxvi.)

495 Christopher Crabtree on the state of paper currency in Scotland [1765].

496 Mr. Crabtree's proposals impracticable [1765].

(Nos. 495, 496 in *Scots Magazine*, xxvii.)

496A Considerations on the present state of the paper money of Scotland [1765].

(*Edinburgh Courant*, February, 1765.)

497 [Swinton, John, Senator of the College of Justice.] A free disquisition concerning the law of entails in Scotland, occasioned by some late proposals for altering the law.
8° Edinburgh 1765.

498 Murray, Patrick, Lord Elibank. Queries relating to the proposed plan for altering the entails in Scotland.
4° Edinburgh 1765.

499 Murray, Patrick, Lord Elibank. Letters on the proposed plan for altering entails in Scotland. Edinburgh 1765.

500 On great and small farms and the corn bounty [1766].
(*Scots Magazine*, xxviii.)

501 [Home, Henry, Lord Kames.] Progress of flax husbandry in Scotland. 8° Edinburgh 1766.

502 [John Maclaurin, Lord Dreghorn.] Considerations on the nature and origin of literary property: wherein that species of property is clearly proved to subsist no longer than for the term fixed by the statute 8vo. Annæ. 8° Edinburgh 1767.

503 Considerations upon the intended navigable communication between the Friths of Forth and Clyde. 4° Edinburgh 1767.

504 Ferguson, Adam. Essay on the history of Civil Society.
4° Edinburgh 1767.

504A Steuart, Sir James. An inquiry into the principles of political economy, being an essay on the science of domestic policy in free nations, in which are particularly considered population, agriculture, trade, industry, money, coin, interest, circulation, banks, exchange, public credit, and taxes.
2 vols. 4° London 1767.

505 [Carlyle, Alexander, D.D., minister of Inveresk.] Essay upon taxes. Particularly tending to shew that the ministers of the Church of Scotland cannot in law, and ought not, in justice and equity, to be subjected to the tax upon houses and lights.
8° 1769.

506 Steuart, Sir James. Considerations on the interest of the County of Lanark, in Scotland.
(Written about 1769, printed in *Collected Works.*)

507 Cassel, J. P. Merkwürdige urkunden eines vertrags zwischen Jakob II. König in Schotland, und der Stadt Bremen.
Bremen 1769.

508 Baldwin, Samuel. A survey of the British customs.
4° London 1770.

509 [Thom, William, minister of Govan.] A letter of advice to farmers, land labourers, and country tradesmen in Scotland, concerning roups of growing corn and of tacks.
8° Glasgow 1771.

510 An inquiry into the late mercantile distresses in Scotland and England; with a few thoughts on the causes of the difficulties . . . of the inhabitants of the whole island.
8° London 1772.

511 An address to the Douglas, Heron & Co. Bank [1772].

512 Remarks on *An Address to the Douglas, Heron & Co. Bank* [1772].

513 On banks established by merchants [1772].

514 A partial relief for our present scarcity of money [1772].
(Nos. 511-514 in *Scots Magazine*, xxxiv.)

515 An abstract of the contract of copartnery of the banking company established in 1769, under the firm of Douglas, Heron & Company Bankers, in Air [1772].

516 Some account of the present stagnation of public credit [1772].

517 Considerations on the present state of public credit [1772].

518 Of our banks, bankers, and public credit [1772].
(Nos. 515-518 in *Scots Magazine*, xxxiv.)

519 Reflections on the Gold Coin Act [1773].
(*Scots Magazine*, xxxv.)

520 Report to the Committee [of the House of Commons] on linen thread in Great Britain and Ireland, 25 May, 1773.
(Reprinted in *Reports from Committees of the House of Commons*, iii.)

521 [Dickson, Rev. Adam, of Whittingham.] An essay on the causes of the present high price of provisions as connected with luxury, currency, taxes, and the national debt.
8° London 1773.

522 [Campbell, Ilay.] Information [addressed to the Lords of Session] for Messrs. Donaldson, Wood, etc., against John Hinton, bookseller, London. 4° Edinburgh 1773.

523 Address to the public by the Society for the Relief of Honest and Industrious Poor in and about the City of Edinburgh, Dec. 22, 1773.
(*Scots Magazine*, xxxv.)

524 Present state of the Edinburgh charity workhouse [1773].
(*Scots Magazine*, xxxv.)

525 Loch, David. Curious and entertaining letters concerning the trade and manufactures of Scotland, particularly the woolen and linen manufactures . . . likewise a plan of the public in order to reduce the prices of the necessaries of life.
3rd ed. 8° Edinburgh 1774.

526 The Scots farmer, or select essays on agriculture, adapted to the soil and climate of Scotland.
2 vols. 8° Edinburgh 1773-4.

527 Campbell, John, LL.D. Political survey of Britain; being a series of reflections on the situation, lands, inhabitants, revenues, colonies, and commerce of this island.
2 vols. 4° London 1774.

528 Loch, David. Letters concerning the trade and manufactures of Scotland, particularly the woollen and linen manufactures.
4° Edinburgh 1774.

529 Snelling, Thomas. A View of the silver coinage of Scotland from Alexander I. to the Union of the two Kingdoms.
Fol. London 1774.

530 Steuart, Sir James. Observations on the new bill for altering and amending the laws which regulate the qualifications of free-holders. 1775.

531 Loch, David. Essays on the trade, commerce, manufactures and fisheries of Scotland; containing remarks on the situation of most of the sea-ports, the number of shipping employed, their tonnage, strictures on the principal inland towns, the different branches of trade and commerce carried on, and the various improvements made in each. 8° Edinburgh 1775.

532 Fea, James. The present state of the Orkney Islands considered.
8° Holyroodhouse 1775.

533 [Arnot Hugo.] A letter to the heritors, farmers, and inhabitants of the county of Edinburgh, to the Lord Provost, magistrates, and town council; the heritors and inhabitants of the city of Edinburgh; and to the heritors and inhabitants of the town of Leith; concerning the establishment of an additional imposition by raising all the tolls in the neighbourhood of the city; and exacting new tolls at the Water-gate and Wester-road to Leith. By a citizen. 8° Edinburgh 1775.

534 [Foulis, Sir James, of Colinton.] Observations on the proposed bridge and bridge-tax: humbly offered to the Town Council of Edinburgh and to the inhabitants of the city and county. 8° Edinburgh 1775.

535 Grod, William. The measurer and tradesman's assistant. 8° Edinburgh 1775.

536 [Murray, Patrick, Lord Elibank.] Eight sets of queries submitted, with an unusual degree of humility, to the nobility, lairds, tenants, etc., of Scotland, upon the subject of wool, and of the woollen manufacture. By a Peer of the Realm. 8° Edinburgh 1775.

537 The History of the Royal Infirmary [of Edinburgh]. 4° [Edinburgh 1776.]

538 Act of the incorporations of Mary's Chapel. Instituting a scheme for providing annuities to widows of the members, passed 8th March, 1768. With obligation of the contributor subjoined. 8° Edinburgh 1776.

539 Yair, Rev. James. An account of the Scotch trade in the Netherlands; and of the staple port at Campvere. 8° London 1776.

540 Home, Henry, Lord Kames. The gentleman-farmer; an attempt to improve agriculture, by subjecting it to the test of rational principles. 8° Edinburgh 1776.

541 Smith, Adam. An inquiry into the nature and causes of the Wealth of Nations. 2 vols. 4° London 1776.

THE MODERN PERIOD FROM 1777 TO 1800.

The last quarter of the eighteenth century was a time of peculiar interest, since it saw the beginnings of a truly scientific study of economic phenomena. Adam Smith's work met with a considerable amount of appreciation, as is shown by the demand for the *Wealth of Nations*. The first edition, as has been shown (No. 541), appeared in 1776, a second in 1778, the third in 1784, the fourth in 1786, and a fifth in 1789. It is significant to note how some of his contemporaries immediately adopted his principles, especially on topics such as the division of labour that were readily apprehended, while on the other hand many others appear quite unaffected by the new influence. Not only so, but the theory of political economy was being developed. An outstanding instance of this is to be found in the works of James Anderson, who, beginning in 1777, established the theory of rent (Nos. 542, 551, 554, 565). This discovery was closely connected with the great attention paid to agriculture and land tenure (Nos. 542, 549, 550, 554, 565, 566, 571, 584, 600, 604, 605, 607, 611, 614-17, 620, 622, 624, 627, 629, 630). Fisheries, too, were dealt with by many writers (Nos. 554, 567, 577, 580, 581, 583, 586, 587, 593, 597, 601, 604, 639), while the coinage, credit and banking—the latter owing partly to the failure of the Ayr Bank—are well represented (Nos. 552, 556, 557-62, 569, 576, 585, 602, 612, 625, 628, 631). Publications became comparatively numerous in the department of taxation and the corn laws (Nos. 546, 547, 553, 574, 603, 609, 610, 623), and the position of the brewing and distilling trade in this connection excited much controversy (Nos. 568, 579, 588-92, 594, 595, 598, 599, 635). Of a more miscellaneous character are tracts relating to manufactures (Nos. 554, 572, 607, 611, 619), to the cloth trade (No. 543), to the regulation of trade by municipalities (Nos. 544, 632-3), to weights and measures (Nos. 563, 564), and to the poor (Nos. 613, 626). It is not without significance that almost at the end of the list there is to be found an indication of nineteenth century conditions—on the one hand, in proposals to mitigate the evils of division of labour (No. 619), and on the other, in an account of an enterprise which still exists, namely, the Carron ironworks (No. 636). Nos. 35, 39, 44, 424 extend into this period.

542 Anderson, James. Essays relating to Agriculture and Rural Affairs. Second edition. 2 vols. 8° Edinburgh 1777.

543 A scheme for establishing and carrying on the woollen manufacture in Dundee. 8° Dundee 1777.

544 The petition of Angus M'Pherson, deacon of the Incorporation of Taylors in Edinburgh; James Murray, deacon of the Incorporation of Taylors of Canongate; and William Rankin, deacon of the Incorporation of Taylors of Potter-row, for themselves and in behalf of the members of said incorporations. 4° [Edinburgh] 1777.

545 Consolatory thoughts on American independence, by a Merchant. Edinburgh 1777.

546 Hutton, Dr. James. Considerations on the nature, quality and distinctions of coal and culm; with inquiries, philosophical and political, into the present state of the laws and the questions now in agitation relative to the taxes on these commodities. 8° Edinburgh 1777.

547 Remarks on *Considerations on the nature, quality, and distinctions of coal and culm, etc.*, by Dr. James Hutton [No. 546]. By a friend of the Revenue. 8° London 1777.

548 Hamilton, Robert. Introduction to merchandise. 2 vols. 8° Edinburgh 1777.

549 [Anderson, James, LL.D.] Miscellaneous observations on planting and training timber-trees, particularly calculated for the climate of Scotland. In a series of letters by Agricola. 8° Edinburgh 1777.

550 Thomson, John. Tables, showing both in Scots and Sterling money, the price of any quantity of grain, etc., from one lippy, or one-fourth part of a peck, to a thousand bolls, at all the various prices from £3 Scots, or 5s. sterling, to £18 Scots, or 30s. sterling. 8° Edinburgh 1777.

551 Anderson, James, LL.D. An inquiry into the nature of the Corn Laws, with a view of the new Corn Bill proposed for Scotland. 8° Edinburgh 1777.

552 [Miller, Patrick, of Dalswinton.] A letter to the proprietors of the Royal Bank of Scotland. 1777.

553 An essay on the Corn Laws, in opposition to the inflamatory memorial for the merchants, etc., of Glasgow. 1777.

554 Anderson, James, LL.D. Observations on the means of exciting a spirit of national industry, chiefly intended to promote the agriculture, commerce, fisheries and manufactures of Scotland. 4° Edinburgh 1777.

555 Barron, William (Professor of Logic at St. Andrews). History of the colonization of the free states of antiquity, applied to the present contest between Great Britain and her American colonies. 4° London 1777.

556 Bank disputes; or credit without abuse. Submitted to the considerate observation of stockholders in the chartered banks of Scotland. 4° Edinburgh 1778.

557 The precipitation and fall of Messrs. Douglas, Heron & Company, late bankers in Air, with the causes of their distress and ruin investigated and considered by a Committee of Inquiry appointed by the proprietors. Edinburgh 1778.

558 Answers for Charles Fergusson & Co., and for Fordyce, Grant & Co., dated 1st May, 1778. [1778.]

559 Wight, Alexander, and Ferguson, Alexander. Letter to the proprietors of Douglas, Heron & Co. [1778.]

560 Fordyce, John. Letters to partners of Douglas, Heron & Co. [1779.]

561 Letter to the partners of Douglas, Heron & Co., by a partner. [1779.]

562 Minutes at a meeting of defenders and doers of defenders in actions at the instance of partners in Douglas, Heron & Co. against the directors. [1780.]

563 [Swinton, John, Senator of the College of Justice.] A proposal for the uniformity of weights and measures in Scotland, by execution of the laws now in force. With tables of the English and Scotch standards, and of the customary weights and measures of the several counties and buroughs of Scotland. Comparisons of the standards with each other, and with the county measures; tables and rules for their reciprocal conversion with each other and with the county measures; and some tables of the weight and produce of corn. 8° Edinburgh 1779.

564 Dalrymple, David, Lord Hailes. Proposals for uniformity of weights and measures in Scotland. 8° Edinburgh 1779.

565 Anderson, James. Inquiry into the causes that have hitherto retarded the advancement of agriculture in Europe. 4° Edinburgh 1779.

566 [Wight, Andrew.] Present state of husbandry in Scotland, extracted from reports made by the commissioners of the annexed estates. 4 vols. 8° Edinburgh 1778-84.

567 On the Scottish fisheries [1781].

(*Scots Magazine*, xliii.)

568 Cunningham, John. An address to the noblemen, etc., proprietors of lands in Scotland, and the inhabitants at large relative to the Scotch brewery. 1781.

569 On bankruptcies [1782].

(*Scots Magazine*, xliv.)

570 Chalmers, George. An estimate of the comparative strength of Great Britain during the present and four preceding reigns; and of the losses of her trade from every war since the Revolution. 8° London 1782.

571 [Ogilvie, William.] An essay on the right of property in land with respect to its foundation in the law of Nature. Its present establishment by the municipal laws of Europe, and the regulations by which it might be rendered more beneficial to the lower ranks of mankind. London 1782.

572 Douglas, Francis. A general description of the east coast of Scotland, from Edinburgh to Cullen, including a brief account of the Universities of Edinburgh and St. Andrews; of the trade and manufactures in the large towns, and the improvement of the country. 12° Paisley 1782.

573 Second report from the Committee [of the House of Commons] appointed to consider the methods practised in making flour and wheat; the prices thereof, and how far it may be expedient to put the same under the regulations of an Assize, 28 May, 1783.

(Reprinted in *Reports from Committees of the House of Commons*, ix. This report relates to Scotland, in the course of which the question of the consumption of grain by distilleries is raised—*c.f.* Nos. 588 to 592.)

574 Steuart, Sir James. A dissertation on the policy of grain. 8° London 1783.

575 Letters, addressed to Sir John Sinclair, Bart., respecting the mode of living, arts, commerce, literature, manners, etc., of Edinburgh in 1763, and since that period. Illustrating the statistical progress of the capital of Scotland.
8° Edinburgh 1783.

576 King, John. Thoughts on the difficulties and distresses in which the peace of 1783 has involved the people of England; on the present disposition of the English, Scots, and Irish to emigrate to America. 8° London 1783.

577 Anderson, James, LL.D. The true interest of Great Britain considered, or a proposal for establishing the northern British fisheries. 12° 1783.

578 Dalrymple, John. Address and proposals on the subject of coal, tar, and iron branches of trade. 8° Edinburgh 1784.

579 Reports from the Committee [of the House of Commons] on illicit practices used in defrauding the revenue, 24 December, 1783; 1 March, 1784; 23 March, 1784.
(Reprinted in *Reports from Committees of the House of Commons*, xi.)

580 Knox, John. A view of the British Empire, more especially of Scotland; with proposals for the improvement of that country, with the extension of its fisheries, and the relief of the people. 2 vols. 8° London 1784.

581 Reports from the Committee [of the House of Commons] appointed to enquire into the state of the British fisheries and the most effectual means for this improvement and extension, 11 May, 1785; 27 June, 1785; 14 July, 1785.
(Reprinted in *Reports from Committees of the House of Commons*, x. Adam Smith was one of the witnesses before this Committee.)

582 Anderson, James, LL.D. Account of the state of the Hebrides and the western coast of Scotland, in which an attempt is made to explain the circumstances that have hitherto repressed the industry of the natives. 8° Edinburgh 1785.

583 M'Cullough, Lewis. Observations on the herring fisheries upon the south and east coasts of Scotland. 8° London 1786.

584 [Ogilvie, W., Professor of Latin at Aberdeen.] An essay on the right of property in land, with respect to its foundation in the law of Nature; its present establishment by the municipal laws of Europe; and the regulations by which it might be rendered more beneficial to the lower ranks of mankind.
8° London [? 1786.]

585 Cardonnel, Adam de. Numismata Scotiæ, or a series of the Scottish coinage from the reign of William the Lion to the Union. 4° Edinburgh 1786.

586 Knox, John. Observations on the northern fisheries; with a discourse on the expediency of establishing fishing stations, or small towns, in the Highlands of Scotland and Hebride Islands. To which is added the last report of the Committee appointed by the House of Commons to enquire into the state of the British fisheries. 8° London 1786.

587 The necessity of founding villages contiguous to harbours, for the effectual establishment of fisheries on the west coast of Scotland and the Hebredies. 8° London 1786.

588 Ross, Walter, Writer to the Signet. The present state of the distillery of Scotland. Edinburgh 1786.

589 The grievances of the distillers of Scotland [1786].
(*Scots Magazine*, xlviii.)

590 Truths, in answer to the facts published respecting the Scottish distillery. Edinburgh 1786.

591 Resolutions of the landed interest of Scotland respecting the distillery; with reasons why the duty upon British spirits should be levied by an annual licence upon the still, respecting its contents. 8° Edinburgh 1786.

592 Observations on the distillery. [? 1786.]

593 Fea, James, Surgeon. Considerations on the fisheries in the Scotch islands; with a general account elucidating the history, soil, products, curiosities, etc., of the same.
8° London 1787.

594 Case for the capital corn distillers of Scotland; containing objections to a bill prepared to be presented to Parliament, entitled "A bill for discontinuing the former duties on low wines and spirits, for granting other duties in lieu thereof."
London 1787.

595 Case of the distillers of corn spirits in North Britain.
London 1787.

596 Knox, John. A tour through the Highlands of Scotland and the Hebride Isles in 1786. 8° London 1787.

597 Fea, James, Surgeon. Considerations on the fisheries in the Scotch islands; with a general account elucidating the history, soil, productions, curiosities, etc., of the same.
8° London 1787.

598 [MacDonald, Thomas.] A review of the laws and regulations respecting the distillery of Scotland. 8° London 1788.

599 Answers for the corn distillers in Scotland to the memorial of the corn distillers in London, presented to the Lords Commissioners of His Majesty's Treasury. 1788.

600 Dickson, Adam. The husbandry of the ancients.
8° Edinburgh 1788.

601 Dempster, George, of Dunichen. A discourse, containing the proceedings of the Society for Extending the Fisheries and Improving the Sea-coasts of Great Britain, and thoughts on the present emigrations from the Highlands; with reflections by John Gray. 8° London 1789.

602 Warrants of the charters erecting, confirming, and granting new privileges to the Royal Bank of Scotland.
8° Edinburgh 1789.

603 Case of the trading interest of Scotland; exhibiting a remarkable instance of discrimination in the corn bill now under the consideration of Parliament. s. sh. Fol. London 1790.

604 Naismith, John. Thoughts on various objects of industry pursued in Scotland. 8° Edinburgh 1790.

605 State of sheep farming on the east coast of Scotland [1791].
(*Scots Magazine*, liii.)

606 Newte, Thomas. Prospectus and observations or in tour in England and Scotland, natural, economical, and literary.
4° London 1791.

607 Sinclair, Sir John. The statistical account of Scotland, drawn up from the communications of the ministers.
21 vols. 8° Edinburgh 1791-9.

608 Ferguson, Adam. Principles of moral and political science.
Edinburgh 1792.

609 Anderson, James, LL.D. Observations on the effect of coal duty upon the remote and thinly peopled coasts of Britain.
8° Edinburgh 1792.

610 Considerations on the present scarcity and high price of coals in Scotland; and on the means of procuring greater quantities at a cheaper rate. With an appendix containing some observations on the laws relative to salt; on those imposing a duty on coal carried coastwise; and on the laws relating to the distillery in Scotland. 8° Edinburgh 1793.

611 Heron, Robert. Observations made in a journey through the western counties of Scotland, in 1792; relating to the scenery, antiquities, customs, manners, population, agriculture, manufactures, commerce, etc. 2 vols. 8° Perth 1793.

612 Anderson, James, LL.D. Thoughts on the privileges and power of juries, with observations on the present state of the country with regard to credit. 8° Edinburgh 1793.

613 Anderson, James, LL.D. Remarks on the poor law in Scotland. 4° Edinburgh 1793.

614 Maxwell, Robert. Select transactions of the Society of Improvers of Agriculture in Scotland. 8° Edinburgh 1793.

615 Anderson, James. A practical treatise on peat moss, considered as in its natural state fitted for affording fuel, or as susceptible of being converted into mold capable of yielding abundant crops of useful produce. 8° Edinburgh 1794.

616 Collection of reports, containing a general view of the agriculture of various counties in Scotland, drawn up by the Board of Agriculture.
5 vols. 4° Edinburgh and London 1793-95.

617 Donaldson, James. Modern agriculture; or the present state of husbandry in Great Britain.
4 vols. 8° Edinburgh 1795-96.

618 On the trade of Great Britain [1796].
(*Scots Magazine*, lviii.)

619 Observations on the objections against machines to shorten labour; with some important considerations on the duties of manufacturers respecting the health and morals of their workmen [1796].
(*Scots Magazine*, lviii.)

620 Naismith, John. Observations on the different breeds of sheep, and the state of sheep farming in the southern districts of Scotland. 4° Edinburgh 1795.

621 [Campbell, John.] Address to the free holders of Scotland, on the legality and effects of a revaluation of landed property.
8° Edinburgh 1795.

622 Anderson, James. Recreations in Agriculture, Natural History.
1799-1802.

623 [Bell, Benjamin.] Observations on the assessment of tolls as a public revenue, to which are added calculations on the probable amount of some other articles of taxation, less liable to exception. 8° Edinburgh 1797.

624 The invention of the threshing machine, and proposals for rewarding the inventor [1797].
(*Scots Magazine*, lix.)

625 On national wealth and the origin and use of money by a private banker [1797].
(*Scots Magazine*, lix.)

626 Eden, Sir F. M. Bart. The state of the poor; or, a history of the labouring classes in England, from the Conquest to the present period; in which are particularly considered, their domestic economy, with respect to diet, dress, fuel and habitation; and the various plans which from time to time have been proposed and adopted for the relief of the poor.
3 vols. 4° London 1797.
(In an appendix there is an account of the poor in Scotland.)

627 Report from the Committee [of the House of Commons] appointed to take into consideration the means of promoting the cultivation and improvement of waste, uninclosed and unproductive lands and the common arable fields, common meadows, and commons of pasture in this Kingdom, 27 April, 1797.
(Reprinted in *Reports from Committees of the House of Commons*, ix.)

628 [Heron, Robert.] A letter from Ralph Anderson, Esq., to Sir John Sinclair, Bart., M.P., etc., on the necessity of an instant change of ministry and an immediate peace: in order to renew the circulation of coin, to revive public and private credit, and to save the British constitution from utter ruin.
8° Edinburgh 1797.

629 Communications to the Board of Agriculture on subjects relative to the husbandry and internal improvements of the country.
7 vols. 4° London 1797-1811.

630 Jix, William Spicer. Remarks on the utility of a new invented patent machine for clearing grain from the straw.
4° London 1797.

631 Conder, James. An arrangement of provincial coins, tokens, and medalets, with a preface by James Wright, of Dundee.
2 vols. 4° Ipswich 1798.

632 Reply by Mr. Smith to *The Answer of the Town Council* to his address, containing an account of the city's receipt and expenditure for a period of ten years, and other interesting information on the subject of its affairs. 8° Edinburgh 1799.

633 Letters of correspondence between the magistrates of Edinburgh and the late Provost Elder. Answers to Thomas Smith, Esq., by the old magistrate and impartial citizen, with notes and observations on each. Also an account of the Edinburgh ale duty from the commencement of the tax.
8° Edinburgh 1799.

634 Reports from the Committee [of the House of Commons] appointed to inquire into the state of the herring fishery and the most effectual means for their improvement and extension, 5 April, 1798; 27 June, 1798; 22 December, 1798; 19 March, 1799; 12 May, 1800.
(Reprinted in *Reports from Committees of the House of Commons*, x.)

635 Reports from the Committee [of the House of Commons] appointed to examine the matters contained in several papers, which were presented to the House upon February 21st last [1798], relative to the distilleries in Scotland, 11 June, 1798; 12 July, 1799.
(Reprinted in *Reports from Committees of the House of Commons*, xi.)

636 Account of the Carron Foundry [1799].
(*Scots Magazine*, lxi.)

637 Girvin, John. The impolicy of prohibiting the exportation of rock-salt from England to Scotland, to be refined there (illustrated). 8° London [1799.]

638 [Bruce, John.] Report on the events and circumstances which produced the Unions of the Kingdoms of England and Scotland; on the effects of this on the reciprocal interests of both Kingdoms; and on the political and commercial influence of Great Britain. 2 vols. 8° [London 1799.]

639 Girvan, John. A short account of the herring fishery in the Frith of Forth; with sundry remarks and general observations.
8° London, reprinted Edinburgh 1800.